Relationship Reruns:

How To Break The Cycle Of Choosing The Wrong People For The Right Relationships

Tanya White

AAA PUBLISHING

AWESOME AUTHORS IN ACTION
DELIVERING STAR QUALITY READING SATISFACTION

Relationship Reruns: How To Break The Cycle Of Choosing The Wrong People For The Right Relationships

Published By Awesome Authors In Action Publishing, LLC (AAA Publishing, LLC)
P.O. Box 16635, Louisville, KY 40256

Awesome Authors In Action, Delivering Star Quality Reading Satisfaction

Details in some illustrations and stories have been changed and or slightly exaggerated to protect the identities of the persons involved.

ISBN 978-0-9816-8470-3

Library of Congress Control Number: 2008904211

Printed in the United States of America

2008-First Edition

To my nephew Trey and niece Emory
Always be wise about choosing your relationships.
You deserve nothing less than God's best.
So refuse to settle and you will soar high in life.

Aunt Tee loves you both!

Acknowledgements

To God, whose unconditional and unending love has saved and redeemed me not only from the snares of Satan but from my self inflicted drama and self sabotaging behavior. Thank you Lord for your grace and mercy.

Also, to my late parents Joe Louis White Sr. (1944-1996) and Erma Jean White (1946-2005) who taught me the power of family, faith and focus. Thank you both for your sacrifice, strict rules and saturation of unconditional love. I am the woman that I am because of it. Love and miss you both so much.

Thanks to my sister L'Dawn and brother Joe for all the talks and nuggets of wisdom that keep my creative juices flowing. Keep speaking truth to me even when I strongly disagree.

To Trey and Emory thanks for keeping your Aunt Tee grounded to what is truly important in life. I am always praying for your life long healthiness and success. Love you both.

To Reverend Syvoskia Bray and WEN Ministries, thank you for allowing me to exercise my spiritual gifts.

To my girl Chelly Chele of Waukegan, Illinois. Remember you are a Rolex girl! Everybody can not afford you and those who can, must be willing to pay the price. Refuse to settle for a prince when the King of Kings has your king waiting to usher you into your queendom.

To all of my coworkers, mentors and friends who listen to my big dreams and believe that I can achieve them.

To all of my awesome Tanya's Tips newsletter subscribers. Not long ago, my writing was just a flickering hobby that encouraged a small group of people in my church community. But now, because of your willingness to share the weekly issues with others, my writing is a large flame of hope that empowers people throughout the world! Thank you so much for your support.

To every person who will read or even hear about this book, thank you allowing me to share nuggets of wisdom with you. I have an authentic passion to empower you with the truth. The truth really does set you free. Be free to have healthy, whole and productive relationships. You deserve the best and nothing less.

Table of Contents

Relationship Pre-Run:
The Awakening

"Tanya, I know how much you are against relationships."
"I am not against relationships," I strongly debated. "What I
am against is dating the wrong person for the wrong reasons."

This was the dialogue that I engaged in one fall night over dinner with a friend. My friend's statement, while shocking and somewhat disheartening, surprisingly struck a nerve so deep within me that it forced me to do an unexpected, but necessary, self-check. Feeling compelled to rectify any misinterpretations that my friend had concerning my dating philosophy, I immediately embarked on another journey of personal awakening and refinement.

Honestly, unbeknownst to my friend, for the next several weeks, I was spiraling into an emotional state of total confusion. Although extremely private and discreet when it comes to dating situations, I thought it was apparent to my friend that I was the quintessential

1

romantic. I believe in being in love. I am open to the idea of marriage and all the great milestones that will occur after entering into that long lasting commitment. So why did my friend believe that I was against being in a relationship? Was I really against dating as they assumed? Had I been subtly giving the message that I was a lifelong advocate for staying single? Did my many years of teaching Christian singles on how to have holy, healthy and wholesome relationships with God, themselves and other people inadvertently transfer into me being the president of an imaginary "Stay Single" nationwide anti-dating campaign? Maybe what my friend proclaimed at dinner that night had some validity.

I knew that facing some hard truths about my past dating relationship attitudes and patterns was the key to solving this mystery. Subsequently, after several unscheduled counseling sessions, some intense and truthful spiritual guidance, as well as weeks of uninterrupted mediation and self-reflection, my total state of confusion to my friends' statement began to subside. I concluded that regardless of the fact that I was still healing from some lingering issues of rejection, certain insecurities and fears of various kinds; in actuality, I was not against dating. Nor was I the poster child for lifelong singleness. And as for the nationwide "Stay Single" anti-dating campaign, well that may have been either a misinterpretation or justification for their personal attitudes that were contradictory to my spiritual beliefs concerning Christian holiness, healthiness and wholeness.

My friend had mistaken my dating boundaries and expectations as me being against relationships. My unwillingness to settle for less than God's best for me was ammunition for them to try to attack my dating philosophy. The audacity of me to exhibit strong personal, spiritual and emotional integrity by refusing to date the wrong person for the sake of having companionship was inconceivable to them.

It is truly amazing how a small statement could lead to a huge personal quest for enlightenment and improvement. My friends' innocent divine dinner declaration served as an emotional and social Milk of Magnesia which cleansed the toxins that were affecting every relationship decision in my life. In addition to scrutinizing my attitudes and actions about dating, I had to analyze other relationships in my life such as friendships, Christian connections, work relationships and business associations.

The goal of this book is to help you transform your negative relationship mindset and actions. Hence, if you want changed relationships then you must have changed actions. If you want changed actions then you must have changed thinking. Throughout this book, I will serve as your special facilitator of change by focusing on the five categories of relationships: love connections, friendships, Christian connections, work related relationships and business associations.

I will use thought provoking insight, personal relationship examples and real life situations, which have been used with permission in which the names have been changed and or slightly exaggerated. As I reveal some uncomfortable truths and share some dreadful consequences about what happens as a result of choosing the wrong people for the right relationships, it is my prayer that the alarms start to ring loud and clear in your rerun situations. If by chance one of the relationship examples is a direct reflection of your situation, then rest assured that it is a divine sign from God.

After reading this book, I hope that you develop the patience to find healthy, whole and satisfying relationships. My prayer is that you stop playing relationship charades and reach for the fulfilling relationships that you deserve. Do not ignore the pink elephant in your relationships because you may be starving for companionship, friendship or social acceptance. This will only lead you to a cycle of bad relationship decisions.

Relationship Reruns Preview:
Truth and Consequences

"When you analyze the root cause of every deferred dream,
delayed destiny and downward spiral that occurs in your life,
you will discover that you have attached yourself to the wrong
intimate relationship, friendship, business association, Christian
connection or even job situation." —Tanya White

"*I'll be there for you…*" Many evenings around 7:00, 7:30, sometimes 8:00, 11:00 or 11:30 p.m., you can catch me repeating this upbeat chorus as I prepare to become mesmerized by the reruns of my favorite show *Friends*. Now, believe me when I tell you that I absolutely L-O-V-E, love, love, love *Friends*! I have a T-shirt with the entire cast on the front. I have the series finale commemorative magazine. In my office, I have a wall portrait of Joey, Phoebe, Ross, Rachel, Chandler and Monica staring directly at me. I have even transferred my exhilarating enthusiasm for the show onto my ten-year-old nephew Trey who can be heard occasionally singing the *Friends* theme song too.

4

I gladly call myself a *Friends* fanatic! At least once a month, I have my own personal *Friends* marathon weekend where I watch the extended versions of all ten seasons I have in my special, untouchable *Friends* DVD collection.

I know what you are thinking. Why do I watch the reruns faithfully when I have all of the shows on DVD? Honestly, I have no answer. Maybe it is because the show makes me laugh uncontrollably. Or maybe it is because I have an unusual sense of peace and contentment when I am drawn into their imaginary lives for thirty minutes.

But whatever the reasons for my *Friends* addiction, I am willfully investing valuable time watching these reruns. I am laughing at scenes I have seen before and can recite verbatim. I sit planted waiting for Joey to say something different when that is an impossible expectation. I long for Ross and Rachel not to break up after he has a one night stand with the copy center girl in the third season. I have brief moments of frivolous emotional escapes and the security of sameness when I am engulfed in these reruns.

Yet, when the fun has ceased, I am no longer being entertained or I have to attend to some issues in my life, I have no other choice but to snap back into reality. I realize that my wishing, cheering and hoping for a changed outcome will never happen. I can pitch a different script idea to the producers however nothing is going to change because I have put my faith in a rerun. I can make excuses to fit what I really want, cry perpetually and throw the longest temper tantrum but I have to come to terms with the fact that I am watching a rerun. I can even pray in my heavenly language and fast for forty days, but the episode is never going to change because I am engrossed in a rerun.

Sadly, my *Friends* fetish is similar to many peoples' relationship habits. As I am glued to my reruns of *Friends*, so many people are whisked away on an emotional roller coaster of what I have penned in this book, relationship reruns. Month after month, year after year, relationship after relationship, many individuals waste precious time choosing to be in a perpetual cycle of unwanted, unsatisfying and unhealthy relationships.

In his book, *Maximize Your Edge: Navigating Life's Challenges,* Dr. Lance D. Watson of Richmond, Virginia, stresses that no one can proceed to live their lives with passion without authentic, meaningful, mature and Godly social relationships. Relationships are needed for our personal growth and fulfillment. God even said it is not good for us to be alone. All relationships are relevant and right for us to live a purposeful life. However, choosing the wrong people for the right relationships disrupts our peace, productivity and purity.

Now, I must admit that I wasted many years settling for repeated cycles of my own relationship reruns. But, I have discovered that at the root of my unfavorable choices were negative self-esteem, low confidence and an unawareness of my divine identity and purpose. As Reverend Syvoskia Bray preached in her sermon, *It's What You Crave,* I yearned for deliverance but my unhealthy emotional cravings for acceptance and love overpowered my ability to make sound relationship decisions. It was not until I recognized that every deferred dream, delayed destiny and downward spiral that occurred in my life was a direct result of my connecting with the wrong people for the right reasons.

"We rise to high positions or remain at the bottom because of conditions we can control if we desire to control them," is what Napoleon Hill proclaims in his classical inspirational book, *Think and Grow Rich.* One of those conditions that we have complete autonomy over is our relationships. Nevertheless, many of us gladly relinquish that control and connect with people who add sorrow, stagnation and strife instead of significance to our lives.

But why do we subject ourselves to intentional misery? Why do we invest time in an unwanted relationship just for the sake of not being lonely? Why do we suppress long-term satisfaction for the sake of grabbing short-term gratification? How is it that we are continuously compelled to fall prey to unhealthy relationships that destroy our self esteem, physical bodies, financial security or zest for life? These and many other truths will be revealed throughout this book with the perfect combination of unique practicality, humor and honesty.

Relationships are influential in you defining who you are, shaping your dreams, sharing your sacred emotions and living out your purpose. God designed every relationship to become a beautiful instrument in the symphony of life. Yet, relationship reruns tend to weigh us down with S.I.N. (S.I.N. is an acronym for Self Inflicted Nonsense, as stated in a sermon by Dr. Lance D. Watson). Continuously entertaining the wrong relationships can literally kill your progress and vitality in life. If your relationships are not encouraging you to be everything God created you to be, then you clearly have attached yourself to the wrong people for the right reasons.

Series 1:
Love Connections

"The first step towards change is admitting that you have a problem."
—Dr. Phil McGraw, Love Smart

L-O-V-E! We all want it. We all need it. Once we find love, it is exciting and exhilarating. A healthy love connection does exactly what R&B sensation Beyoncé Knowles sings about in her song *Upgrade You.* A genuine love connection is a balanced upgrade of mind, money and motivation. It does not cause you, or the other party involved, to feel any shame or regret for being in the relationship. A real love is not forced, faked and entered into frivolously.

A certain level of emotional security and higher level of self confidence illuminates from every fabric of your body when you have a healthy love connection. Shame does not knock at your door when you are dating the right person. You become allergic to masquerades, moral compromise and minimizing your self worth. Connecting to the right kind of love is like cooling water that quenches your thirst on a steamy July day.

On the other hand, bad relationship choices compel you to drift further away from obtaining authentic happiness. Love connections quickly transform into devastating disconnections when you allow the wrong person access to your life. But, the dating drama can cease when you understand the root causes for your vicious cycle of reruns, refuse to date down and commit to applying the R-E-S-T strategy at every stage of the relationship's development.

Episode 1:
The Roots Of Your
Relationship Reruns:
Why Do Fools Fall In Love?

"Romantic love is the only life state that triggers the same intense need for completeness and connectedness that we experience as children. . .We unconsciously choose mates who reflect the positive and negative qualities of our original caretakers in order to resolve the unfinished business from our childhood." —Dr. Robin L. Smith, Lies at the Altar

In January 1977, approximately 130 million people watched, for eight consecutive nights, as Alex Haley took us on a cleverly engaging journey tracing his family lineage back to the 1767 origination of his African heritage. A generation was inspired and reminded of the society's struggle in the timeless television adaptation of his best-selling book *Roots*. Although I had just turned six, I can remember the excitement that was felt when *Roots* aired.

This movie was the topic of concern during many conversations that my parents had with their friends. Because it was an annual television event for almost ten years, my household, and many households across the nation, received a piece of African American history via mainstream media as *Roots* compelled us to search through our past in order to understand our present and prepare for our future.

Like Alex Haley, you too must discover your roots in order for you to have healthy relationships. If you have realized that you keep having the same type of relationship with different people for 1, 3, 5, 10 years or more, then you have to admit that you are the only common dominator. There may be unresolved hurts, unaddressed fears and insecurities that are driving your repeated wrong relationship decisions.

In the majority of your relationships, are you constantly asking the questions: What in Hades am I doing trying to pursue a relationship with this person? How did I get in this predicament again with someone I really have nothing in common? When you are trapped in a vicious pattern of relationship reruns you tend to look for love in all the wrong places. You look for love in too many faces without the thought of discussing compatibility, shared values or relationship history. You dive into the relationship head first and become a fool in love. But why do fools really fall in love?

As I stated earlier, God wired humans to be in relationships. In 1943, Abraham Maslow proposed that all humans are motivated in life through a series of five hierarchical needs. His theory gives a bottom up approach to these hierarchies of needs, which ultimately drives a person to reach the pinnacle of psychological wholeness. You will only reach the higher levels of this pyramid when the lower needs are satisfied.

According to www.wikipedia.org, Maslow's five needs consist of the following:

LEVEL	NEED	EXPLANATION
1st Level	Physiological	This level includes the needs of having food, water, clothing, breathing, sleep and sex.
2nd Level	Safety	Being secure in having employment, resources, morality, family, health and property.
3rd level	Love/ Belonging	Family, friendships and sexual intimacy are important to fulfill this level. Notice the sex mentioned in Level 1 is different from sexual intimacy at this level. These two different needs will be discussed later in Chapter One.
4th Level	Esteem	This embodies self-esteem, confidence, achievement, respecting others and expecting others to respect you.
5th Level	Self-actualization	This is the highest and considered to be the healthiest level to achieve. At this level, you are actively pursuing morality, being your authentic self, solving the problems in your life without avoidance or escape, freeing yourself from all prejudice and accepting as well as living by truth.

Sadly, a vast majority of people are paralyzed at the third level of the hierarchy of needs. If you are stuck at the third level of the hierarchy of needs, then your quest to experience a sense of belonging is camouflaged by forcing love connections that are not healthy or satisfying. What you have convinced yourself of as being love unfortunately is just a pseudo relationship of convenience, which temporarily tickles surface level emotions instead of satisfying the inner parts of your soul. Many relationships of convenience quickly turn into emotional and mental poison which eventually infects every facet of your life.

Can You Handle It?

"You Can't Handle The Truth!" Jack Nicholson made this statement infamous in the 1992 Oscar nominated hit movie *A Few Good Men.* You may not have seen the movie, but I know that you have heard his line recited a million times or more. Honestly, I sometimes watch the movie just to see that scene.

In fact, people remember that movie not because it had an all-star cast starring such acting legends as Tom Cruise, Demi Moore or Cuba Gooding, Jr. Nor do people automatically recall the movie because it had an amazing storyline. On the contrary, this movie is remembered for Jack Nicholson screaming at Tom Cruise, *"You Can't Handle The Truth!"*

Even though people say they want to hear it, the truth is avoided like the bubonic plague. Why is that? Because once digested, the truth purges you of the toxic waste that has been stopping your life from flowing properly. Basically, once you are confronted with the truth it forces you to change, and frankly change makes people panic.

In her best selling book, *Lies at the Altar*, Dr. Robin L. Smith writes, *"People often tell me that changing old ways seems hard. But there is*

13

nothing more draining than trying to force a relationship into "happily ever after" when the truth is an unwelcome guest in your home." You must embrace change because change is inevitable. Everything changes. Seasons change. Attitudes change. Organizations change. Relationships change. You can not afford to be afraid to change.

People who are afraid of change are usually afraid of the truth. It is easier for them to live in a state of fantasy, aloofness or being oblivious to the actuality of reality than to live a life of unadulterated truth. For years I have always said that, *"Truth is something everyone says they tell, many say they want to hear, but very few actually live by."* Yet, if you are not living by truth, it is difficult for you to hear it and next to impossible for you to expect it in your relationships.

Subjecting yourself to an unbreakable cycle of relationship reruns is like what Bill Murray experienced in the 1993 unexpected hit comedy movie *Groundhog Day*. According to the movie details from Wikipedia, Murray played a news anchor stranded in a small town reporting the Groundhog Day celebrations. After what turned out to be one of the worst days of his life, to much of his dismay and frustration, Murray became trapped in an unending time loop of repeating the same day, over and over again.

After becoming accustomed to the same expectations and outcomes, Murray began to indulge in harmful activities. Since his life seemed to be stuck on the repeat button, he concluded that his actions were not going to have any long-term consequences. The resolution came only when Murray allowed wise counsel to deliver him from the dreadful cycle by putting a strategy into place. He changed his approach and enhanced his overall outlook to his life. Once Murray changed his approach, he experienced a brand new day in his life.

Why do you keep accepting the lead role in your self inflicted *Groundhog Day* experience? How do you continuously find yourself in unwanted, unsatisfying or unhealthy relationships? How will your season of reruns end?

Like Murray, your relationship reruns will stop when you invite a trusted source who is free from hidden motives, intimidation or irrationality into your intimate circle. By reading this book, you have extended the invitation to me to be that trusted source. I intend to be the voice of truth and the vehicle of change to help usher you to a brand new season of healthy love connections. The remainder of this chapter will list some root causes as to why you are trapped in a vicious cycle of relationship reruns.

You Are Tired Of "Living Single"

According to the 2006 U.S. Census Bureau statistics, of the 238,585,682 people in America, ages 15 and over, a 49.7% or about 118,577,084 people are single (single meaning not married). That is almost half the population! Check out the break down of the 49.7% men and women age 15 and over who are single in the U.S., as reported by the 2006 Census Bureau statistics:

Category of Singleness	%
Single by divorce	10.5
Single by separation	2.3
Single by death of a spouse	6.4
Single and never been married	30.5

Since being single is still taboo in today's society (especially if you are a woman), many shows and movies center around the dilemmas of dating. The 1990's television hit *Living Single* cleverly stuck to this relationship recipe. The show centered around six African American thirty-something friends (four women and two men) who struggled with finding the perfect mate.

Even though the show stressed the characters' drive for career success and healthy friendships, ultimately every episode would address one of the character's desires to have Mr. or Ms. Right. Particularly, the character of Regine (played by Kim Fields) would continuously get cross-examined by her mother about the absence of a husband. It would lead to her mother asking the infamous question, "When are you going to get married so that I can have some grandchildren?"

As one of the 49.7% of singles in the U.S., I could definitely identify with Regine's frustration. I used to frequently receive the same barrage of questions from family and friends about getting married. People still thought that women were to graduate high school, go to college to find a husband, get hitched and start popping out babies. If you were not on the marriage track as a young woman then you would inevitably have to combat the silent whispers of "Something must be wrong with her" or the misconceptions that you are against relationships because you were single.

I remember forcing myself into several unwanted, unsatisfying and, on a couple of occasions, unhealthy love connections to escape the grueling questioning at family functions. We were either incompatible socially, economically, emotionally, spiritually or all of the above. One or both of us would camouflage true relationship needs in public. But behind close doors we were always frustrated, arguing or having episodes of quiet tension. When the relationship had eventually run its course, I always had some type of regret.

Thank the Lord when I entered "thirtydom" I finally woke up to the reality of life and relationships. First, I had to realize that being alone did not mean that I was lonely. I had to undergo a painful and massive transformation of self discovery and self appreciation. I started viewing my singleness as a blessing and a time of enlightenment. If I had conformed to the pressures of society and gotten married prematurely, I am 300% sure that I would be divorced because I was completely clueless as to who I was.

Whenever you are tired of living single and viewing singleness as a disease then in your mind the only solution is having a companion. A prolonged sense of urgency begins to taunt your every thought and action. As a response to this anxiousness to find companionship, you adopt a "by any means necessary" philosophy. You will start grabbing hold to meaningless encounters with people you have nothing in common with.

In this state, compromising your integrity or spiritual belief mysteriously becomes your new life standard. Even dating someone who is married may inadvertently become acceptable and excusable in your eyes. Sexual escapades with people you hardly know will be your new approach to building a long lasting commitment. You seem not to mind giving someone complete access to your head, heart and home for the simple fact that you have become allergic to living the single life. Your relationship theme song ironically becomes Luther Ingram's 1972 ballad, *If Loving You Is Wrong, I Don't Wanna Be Right*. Whenever your desire for companionship supersedes your practical wisdom and common sense, then the sweet life you once knew transforms into a nightmare on Elm Street.

During my phases of trying to escape the single life, I was foolishly convincing myself that accepting any kind of love connection was better than having nothing at all. I would always justify blatant relationship incompatibilities by telling myself a few internal lies such as:

17

▶ Nobody's perfect. I need to be more open and decrease my high standards.

▶ He is not all that bad. We can make this work.

▶ We are just friends. Nothing serious.

▶ It is better to have somebody than nobody.

▶ I know this relationship is not in God's will, but He knows my heart.

▶ I am so tired of being alone.

I do not care how many excuses you give, pursuing dead-end relationships is the loneliest feeling in the world. Having someone in your life but still not feeling fulfilled is emotionally exhausting. You may think that you are having the time of your life by accepting incompatible relationships but the thrill will eventually vanish. Then you must face the harsh reality of dealing with yourself.

Singleness is not a sickness but a choice. You can make a choice to travel down the path of singlehood with patience or to skip down the dark alley of unhealthy relationship compromises. Unfortunately, young and old, Christian and non-Christian, men and women who have selected the latter eventually find themselves curled up beside the relationship dumpster filled with low self esteem, regret and uncertainty.

In his book, *Single, Married, Separated and Life After Divorce,* Myles Munroe writes that in all of the troubled marriages that he counsels, the marriage problems always rest in the fact that two self-haters have joined together to love one another. He continues to write, *"You can only love people to the extent that you love yourself."* To prevent the heartache and shame, which usually follows relationship reruns, it is imperative that you undeniably, unequivocally and unashamedly know and love who you are. A healthy self love requires that you embrace the good, bad and the ugly qualities about yourself. Learning to love yourself is the greatest love that you will ever experience.

To drive the point home, if you want healthy and authentic relationships, you must love yourself first before you try to attempt to love someone else. Remember, no one else is obligated to love you if you do not love yourself. If you are tired of being alone then you are communicating that you are tired of you. And if you are tired of you, then what makes you think that someone else will not get tired of you too?

You Have Been "Waiting to Exhale"

Waiting to Exhale, the national bestselling book and 1995 hit movie written by literary phenomena Terry McMillan, highlights the lives of four African-American women whose stressful life transitions had them seeking solace in the comfort of Mr. Right. The Jerry Maguire fantasy of "you complete me" was the subliminal message these women portrayed during the majority of the movie. These women believed that finding lasting peace and everlasting happiness would only come when the right man entered their life.

The character of Bernadine thought she had her Mr. Right for eleven years, but he eventually left her for his mistress who Bernadine had apparently known about for years. The sexy, savvy and single professional powerhouses, Savannah and Robin seemed too happy about being the magnets for the "married, emotionally unavailable, financially insecure, drug addict" brothers. Gloria, who was the stable entrepreneur and single mother, on the other hand satisfied the absence of male companionship in her life by comforting herself with food. Thankfully, by the end of the movie, these women received

19

the revelation that peace was found by being comfortable in loving themselves and understanding their worth first.

Although this movie is on my list of all time favorites, the disturbing message that someone can bring your life relief and satisfaction is the philosophy that most women and men hold on to their entire lives. When you believe this fallacy, desperation begins to seep from every fabric of your being. Women, the first man who says you are beautiful earns your complete devotion. Men, the woman who strokes your ego in just the right spot can receive monthly financial support. Christian singles who embrace this "waiting to exhale" thinking quickly tend to abandon God's principles and standards to pacify the insatiable cravings of becoming a couple.

For example, Celine's waiting to exhale philosophy was intensified when she found herself thirty-nine, unmarried and without children. She was the only female in her family who did not have a husband. It did not matter that ninety-five percent of the couples in her family were unhappy in their unions. Celine desperately wanted to join the elite wives club and finally experience acceptance from the married women in her family. So her focus was to immediately secure a candidate to help thrust her into this high ranking position.

Celine asked all of her girlfriends to become staunch supporters of her "marriage-before-40-campaign" by hooking her up with single bachelors they knew. She had no criteria or standards of what she was looking for in a man. Celine figured that her being thirty-nine and childless no longer gave her any time to have dating standards.

A month later, one of Celine's girlfriends found a candidate. She scheduled a blind dinner date for Celine and Harry. Celine was immediately infatuated with Harry because of his attentiveness toward her the entire night. Compliments flowed. He made her laugh. She had not felt this free with a man since her last relationship ended two years earlier. Just like Whitney Houston's character in the movie, Celine had her "waiting to exhale moment" without knowing any important information about Harry. Celine was confident that she was going to meet her "marriage-before-40-campaign" deadline. So after the blind dinner date, she was determined to do whatever it took to hook Harry forever.

Celine put the relationship into overdrive. She spent all of her free time with him, ignored her social commitments and dropped out of her graduate school program where she was pursuing a Masters degree in Social Work. Within months, she ended her vow of celibacy and began a sexual relationship with Harry, always asking God to forgive her each time they had sex.

In addition, Celine totally ignored the warning signs that Harry needed to focus on getting some areas in his life in order before he could freely pursue a healthy relationship. First of all, a large portion of Harry's income went to paying alimony from his first marriage and child support from his second marriage. He was always months behind paying his bills and had creditors blowing up his phone. Secondly, the engine in his car blew out two weeks after they met. After about a month of Celine letting Harry use her car to run errands and pick up his daughter on the weekends, she eventually cosigned for him to purchase another car in which she gladly paid the note until he straightened out his financial situation.

Lastly, two months after they became an exclusive couple, Harry's department downsized and he lost his job. Although he received a great severance package, he was still in the hole financially. Harry moved in with Celine after he lost his job. To celebrate their new living arrangements, Harry proposed to Celine in which she gladly accepted. The next weekend, Celine went to pick out and purchase her engagement ring. Harry and Celine married one week shy of Celine's 40th birthday. She was ecstatic that her campaign was successful.

Celine was so determined to have MRS. at the beginning of her name that she refused to slow down and address some very important issues that would prohibit marital success. She believed that once they were married everything would magically fall into place. Because she continuously fed her focus, which was to get married, the illusion became next to impossible to break.

Harry did not look for job until about two months before their wedding. But a year later, Harry was unemployed again and depressed because he felt as though no company would hire him because he was in his early fifties. Yet, Celine still refused to discuss her concerns she had with Harry because they were expecting their first child. Although she never admitted it, Celine desperately wished that she would have found another way to exhale. She battled silent depression and regret throughout her entire marriage.

You Are Caught Up In "Sex and the City"

The characters on the show *Sex and the City*, Carrie, Samantha, Miranda and Charlotte, were the fraternal twins of the characters in the movie *Waiting to Exhale*. Underlined with the same theme as *Waiting to Exhale*, these four Manhattan socialites oftentimes predicted the success of their dating relationships on the emotions they experienced during their sexual encounters. But healthy and mature relationships are not sustained through great sex but through experiencing great significance, something these ladies eventually grew to understand.

Pursuing a relationship based on the feelings of sexual ecstasy is absurd. Sex clouds your rationality in relationships. Sexual encounters will have you confusing the magnitude of lustful stimulation with lasting relationship success. Although it can provoke very powerful and potent emotional feelings, sexual intercourse only accounts for a very small percentage of any relationship. Once the act is over, you must get out of bed, pay bills and relate to one another in other ways. Failure to connect financially, spiritually, socially and emotionally jeopardizes the longevity of the relationship. Even today in the midst of HIV, AIDS, the rise of domestic violence cases and so many other detrimental behaviors, people still continue to use sex as the building blocks of a successful love connection.

Because people tend to confuse intimacy with sexuality, they get entangled in a web of lust that turns into deception and eventually they will become lost in gratifying their sexual emotions. Dr. Jamal Harrison-Bryant explains in his book, *Foreplay: Sexual Healing for Spiritual Wholeness*, *"You can not have an intimate relationship with someone you do not know. The most precious and private thing that you possess is your sexuality. Giving your sexuality away sends a signal that you no longer respect or value your most prized possession—yourself."* There still remains a double standard in society that motivates men to define themselves by how many sexual escapades they have while women are chastised if they have the same sexual encounters. But, the truth is that men, as well as women, should value themselves and hold higher sexual standards when it comes to relationships.

How many times have you been blinded by a person you were dating because you engaged in a sexual relationship prematurely? The craziest and most self destructive relationships I had occurred when I confused sex for intimacy. Being young and naïve in my twenties, I thought that the way to get a man to be committed to me was by having sex with him first and then building the relationship from there. If a guy complimented me and said that he was interested in pursuing a relationship with me, then that was good enough for me. It did not matter that I knew nothing about him as a person, his background, past relationship behaviors, if he had any life goals or what his family was like. I was not concerned if he had a job to support himself. If he called me a couple of times, wanted to spend time with me then my next move would usually be to have sex with him to seal the deal.

Sure I would make excuses to justify me rushing into a sexual relationship with someone who was really a stranger. In my mind, I was just getting my needs met and glad that I had a man who showed me attention. So sex was just the next stage of the relationship. I wanted to be loved and I thought the way to get and keep love was through sex. But that was a relationship trap that I willingly set for myself.

You're Hooked to the
"Dreamgirl/Dreamboy" Scene

"And I am telling you..." I think you know the lyrics to this break-up anthem from the timeless Broadway hit play *Dreamgirls,* which later became the blockbuster movie of 2006. This song has misled thousands of people into staying bound to a dead-end relationship. Despite the earth shadowing animated crescendo of determination sung by R&B powerhouse Jennifer (Holiday or Hudson—you take your pick), refusing to leave an unloving and unsatisfying relationship does not save it but creates more self-inflicted chaos.

Honey, when someone does not want you anymore please accept it. Do not resort to begging them to change their mind because you are afraid of being alone. Free yourself. I know the fight to keep a relationship can get your adrenaline pumping but ultimately you can never force a person to love you. Believing that you have the power over people's emotions and actions pushes you toward an emotional breakdown.

There is a show on the Oxygen Channel called *Snapped,* which chronicles the true stories of the lives of women who have been charged with the murder of a loved one, usually a husband. Each story digs deep into the madness which led up to the horrendous murders that these unlikely suspects committed.

With varying circumstances, social, professional and economic backgrounds, all of these women unexpectedly found themselves at the end of their emotional rope. All of the stories address their inability to come to grips with issues such as rejection, disappointment, unresolved past hurt, dishonesty, betrayal, insecurity, infidelity and using material riches as a false sense of security to cover up a deeper issue. As my sister puts it, "These women remind me of a rubber band that is trying to hold too much stuff on the inside. At any moment, the band is going to break and everything that it was holding will scatter everywhere."

People who fall into relationship reruns are like that rubber band, too. When a rubber band is stretched too far from its intended purpose and position, this creates unwanted external tension, which is caused by an excess of internal pressure. Eventually, the pressure from inside the band creates stress on the outside of the band and, at some point, the rubber band snaps.

Now I know that none of us would plan to commit a horrendous act such as murder. But when you have this "dreamgirl/dreamboy" approach to relationships, then there is no telling what you will do. The best strategy for eliminating your chances of having a scene like this is to begin to love those who love you and let go of those who let go of you.

You Are In A "Race To The Altar"

Something old, something new. Something borrowed something blue. In the quest for finding a life long partner, there is a never ending race

25

to have the extravagant wedding complete with all the trimmings. Being able to have the fashionably dressed wedding party, fine food and the opportunity to say "I Do" in front of hundreds of family and friends is an adrenaline rush that will have you sprinting to the chapel to get married. Surprisingly this is such a widespread philosophy that in 2003, NBC actually created a reality show around this concept.

The show comprised of couples who were competing to win the fantasy wedding of their dreams. They were put through a series of challenges designed to test the strength of their relationships. The games involved issues of teamwork, compatibility, compromise, sex, trust, honesty and coping under pressure. Sadly, a vast number of people who choose to fall prey to relationship reruns compete against family, friends and enemies to win the imaginary race to the altar.

Michelle McKinney Hammond suggests in her book, *Get a Love Life*, "*It is the longing to become one with a person that we begin to make adjustments in our own perspectives and priorities.*" Neglecting to invest adequate time in getting to know people on a deeper level is an unhealthy way of fulfilling your cravings for a love connection. Blinded by so many misconceptions, couples are eager to spend large sums of money for an hour celebration instead of taking that same money to seek premarital or even individual counseling to address issues that will inevitably destroy the marriage.

It is amazing to see how intelligent, focused, purpose-driven individuals and even faith-filled Christians throw all common sense out the window when they get a whiff of a relationship that lasts longer than two months. They do not give it a second thought that they are allowing a perfect stranger to have complete access to every area of their emotional, social and spiritual life. Hurried cohabitation, codependency issues and "this is my last chance for romance" philosophy also have couples speeding down the slopes of marriage mountain.

I recall lacing up my track shoes to be the star of my own *Race To The Altar* reality show. I remember dating a guy who was twenty-six, jobless, car-less, and moneyless. He lived with his mother and had two teen-aged daughters. He had zero motivation to find a job let alone keep a job. I, on the other hand, was twenty-three, had a full-time job and had no kids. I was attending the community college part-time. We were clearly on different paths but I thought that somehow our desire to be in a relationship with each other would outweigh our differences.

We would always go out to eat, to the mall, movies and shopping (95% of the time on my dime, of course.) He would call me at work several times during the day because he said he missed me and wanted to know what I was doing. I loved that he called me frequently because it led me to believe that I was the only thing on his mind. But of course I would be because he did not have anything else in his life occupying his time during the day.

I fooled myself into masquerading that I had the perfect relationship. I had a man who showed me a lot of attention and I loved it. No longer was I the topic of the family functions because I had a boyfriend on my arm to show off. I gave him complete access to my life with no questions asked. I even let him drive my car to look for a job a few times, which he did not do. I found out later that he was using my car to drive his babies' mama around town (that is another story for a different section).

And, of course, he said he wanted to marry me. But, why wouldn't he? He did very little in the relationship and he had landed all of my time, talents and treasures. I was supporting him financially and playing step-mom to his two daughters. Do not ask me what I was thinking. I thought I was in love. My family thought he was nice, but I did not dare give them his full statistics. My parents would have had a conniption fit because the relationship was so unbalanced.

How could two people, who obviously were unequally yoked, willingly force a square peg into a round hole? I can not speak for him. However, this was the time when I had very low self-esteem, no confidence and did not know what my purpose was in life. I thought that having a boyfriend would help boost my acceptance level in certain social circles. I convinced myself that when we got married he would get a job and have no other choice but to straighten up. Trying to race to the altar coerced me into burying the truth to myself and everyone around me about this unsatisfying relationship.

Please grab hold to what I am about to say. Whatever you do at the beginning of any relationship shapes the entire relationship. He was not going to find a job after we got married because he did not have one while we were dating. It was impossible to expect that he would provide for his family after the nuptials since he did not provide for his family before I entered the picture. I thank God that He did not allow that relationship to progress any further because I would have been in a loveless, financially stressful, dysfunctional façade of a marriage.

Dr. Robin L. Smith writes in her book, *"We act as if people who are emotionally lifeless, spiritually empty, mean, or selfish are going to transform themselves after the wedding and grow relationship legs."* In reality, the person you see before the wedding is exactly who they are going to be after the wedding. Brothers, if the sister does not maintain a clean house before you say "I do" then marrying you will not magically transform her into Martha Stewart. Sister, if he does not work or have any life goals when you are dating him, then giving him a frequent flyer card to your house, money and goodies, will not motivate him to do any more than he already does. Stop trying to be the quicker fixer upper person because you want to go to the chapel and get married.

Contrary to what the reality show tried to portray, marriage is not a game. It is more than a beautiful ceremony. It is more than receiving a legal spiritual license to have sex. It is not the ultimate cure for loneliness. Marriage is a sacred covenant between two whole and mature people who are equally yoked. They have taken adequate time to discuss important issues concerning family, past hurts, financial status, career and life aspirations, as well as other topics that determine compatibility.

Marriage involves developing intimacy over a long period of time. Most people mistake intimacy for spending lots of time with a person, meeting their friends and family and deciding to date exclusively. Just because you share all of your personal business and are excited about a person does not constitute intimacy. Shannon Ethridge points out in her book, *Every Woman's Battle*, *"Learning new things about a person is not intimacy. Intimacy is seeing what is truly on the inside of a person...Be careful not to mistake intensity for intimacy."*

Do you really know the person you are choosing to date? Are you slowly developing an intimate bond with that person? Do you know who the person is on the inside, in reference to their emotions, mental status and inner thoughts? More importantly, do you know yourself? Remember that you can never have genuine intimacy with another person until you have an intimate awareness of yourself. Slow down. Refuse to become the grand prize winner on your personal reality show called *Race To The Altar*.

You Want To Taste The "Flavor of Love"

Please do not believe the hype that having twenty people fighting for your devotion is a healthy way to finding an everlasting love as the *Flavor of Love* show has seduced millions into believing. Of course when you offer fame and fortune in exchange for being in a relationship, there will be thousands who come to your casting call.

Yet, it will never manifest into the real love that you truly long for or deserve.

Love is not a feeling of uncontrollable exhilarating butterflies in your stomach. That could be gas. Nor is love having your personal smorgasbord of candidates clamoring for your attention. An authentic and healthy loving relationship is a truthful, time consuming investigation to determine if you are compatible with the person.

Bishop George Bloomer gives five ways to know if you are compatible with a potential mate in his book, *Looking For Love*. Bloomer explains that whomever you decide to date and/or marry should have:

▸ Their goals and aspirations aligned with your goals for the future.

▸ You feeling comfortable in their presence instead of having negative anxiety.

▸ The majority of your relationship together free from conflict.

▸ A high regard for living a life of integrity instead of pressuring you to do things that go against your moral judgment.

▸ The ability to resolve conflict in a healthy way without shutting down or blowing up.

Whenever you ignore the warning signs of incompatibility because you like tasting the flavor of love, then you are living a lie. You are capable of discerning warning signs between real love and the lies brought about by the flavor of love. Yet, if you continue to ignore the signs then eventually your lies will become your new truths. Regardless of how long you camouflage the truth, you will ultimately receive the eye-opening revelation that a truth-less relationship welcomes constant chaos, turmoil and confusion.

You Are Stranded On "Fantasy Island"

"The plane! The plane!" From 1978 to 1984, every Saturday night at 10 p.m., after the *Love Boat*, ABC would drop its viewers off on a mysteriously beautiful getaway to *Fantasy Island*. Dressed impeccably in his crisp white suite, Mr. Roarke and his eccentric assistant, Tattoo, would greet people who willingly left the truth of their reality to pay the high price of living out a fantasy. Every guest on the show usually came to the rude awakening that their fantasies brought them a tremendous amount of sadness instead of the intended happiness that they anticipated. By the end of each episode, Mr. Roarke, who warned the guests that their fantasy would bring more harm than good, always stepped in just in the nick of time to reveal the deception of the fantasy and moral lessons.

How many times have you paid hundreds, thousands even millions of dollars to live out some relationship fantasy which was destined to end in disaster? Who was your Mr. Roarke who served as the wise voice of warning so that you could open your eyes to truth? What moral lessons did you learn after the deception of your fantasy was revealed? Before you skip this section, because you feel as though you have never been on *Fantasy Island*, let's get a clear understanding of what a fantasy relationship entails.

According to www.coping.org, a relationship of fantasy can be described as one of the following:

▶ Unrealistic, unattainable expectations in which you require others to meet in order for you to feel happy, content, and satisfied.

▶ A relationship used as an escape, a sanctuary, and a refuge to which your mind can flee when you have problems, conflicts, or disappointments.

▶ A daydream created because you are experiencing a painful, abusive, or neglectful relationship. By escaping into fantasy you avoid dealing with the problems. The tasks necessary to bring the relationship into reality are avoided.

▶ A relationship more active in your subconscious than in your conscious mind. It can be the root of your unhappiness with your real relationships.

▶ A three dimensional reality when you meet a person who matches some or all of your criteria for the fantasy. The object of your fantasy may enter a clandestine relationship of the mind, heart, or flesh (especially if you are married). This fantasy makes you acutely aware of how inadequate your current relationship is, even though the new person is neither attainable nor is there a future for the relationship.

▶ An emotional block, intellectual barrier or the actual immobilizer that keeps you from becoming committed to working out your current relationship.

But despite all of the above, the most important indicator that you are not in a relationship of fantasy is that both parties are actively participating, nurturing and maturing the relationship. Relationships are not a one woman or one man show. They are an open and active dialogue of commitment between people who have the same relationship purpose and expectations.

The experts at www.coping.org explain that you should take the time to honestly answer the following questions to determine if you are participating in a fantasy relationship. Ask yourself:

1. Do you blame your partner for real or imagined negligence?

2. Is your partner giving you feedback that you are constantly giving double messages, "damned if you do and damned if you don't" ultimatums, saying one thing and meaning another?

3. Are you chronically daydreaming about the way things "should be" in the relationship?

4. Do you have a tendency to fly off the handle with every little annoying thing your partner does?

5. Do you put your partner in the witness box as the defendant and become a prosecuting attorney asking leading, probing, demanding questions unmercifully?

6. Are you chronically unhappy, depressed, and discouraged whenever you are in your partner's presence even when your partner is committed to trying to work things out with you?

7. Are you finding it difficult to let go of the past mistakes, hurts, and misdeeds of your partner? Are you unable to forgive and forget?

8. Do you resent having to repeat your wants, needs and expectations for the relationship to your partner because you think your partner should already know and be aware of them?

9. Do you seem to discount or ignore the small efforts of change made by your partner on behalf of the relationship?

10. Just when you think you and your partner are going to make it do you find yourself slipping back or relapsing into angry outbursts about minor infractions or errors?

Answering "yes" to one or more of these questions is a red flag that your relationship may be just a fantasy. You should attend to this problem immediately. Usually, when you find yourself in a relationship of fantasy, there are underlying issues of abandonment, rejection, codependency and sometimes emotional and physical abuse.

Relationships of fantasy can have negative consequences in many areas of your life. If you perpetually ignore the root causes of your tendencies to be in fantasy relationships then you are sure to put yourself at risk for one or more of the following, according to www. coping.org.

▶ Chronic depression

▶ Inability to get into a lasting relationship

▶ Inability to make a commitment to anyone in a relationship

▶ One or more divorces

▶ Relationships ending prematurely

▶ Inability to let go of blaming the other

▶ Inability to create a healing environment with your partner

▶ Poor communication with your partner

▶ Competition in your relationship

▶ Chronic conflict, disagreements, and fights

▶ Power struggle for control in your relationship

▶ Lack of intimacy in your relationship

▶ You and/or your partner becoming troubled persons in need of professional help

▶ Emotional problems for you and/or your partner

▶ Inability to accept your partner for who she/he is

▶ Inability to have confidence in your ability to sustain a relationship

▶ Stereotyping all members of the opposite sex or even the same sex.

▶ Loss of trust in your partner

▶ Chronic sense of insecurity

▶ Inability to take a risk

▶ Inability to overcome your fear of entering a committed relationship

▶ Destruction of other relationships

I strongly encourage you to deplane the plane before you become trapped on *Fantasy Island*. It is far less stress to live your own reality than to create a fantasy that will bankrupt your emotions and probably your wallet. Instead, try investing your time and money in counseling or therapy (yes therapy!) to heal from the issues that are causing you to seek fantasy relationships.

You Are A Castaway On "Gilligan's Island"

Failure to venture out of your comfort zone will have you desiring and attracting the same type of people. Just like the castaways on *Gilligan's Island*, when you are stuck on your own island of isolation, looking at the same scenery and talking to the same people day in and day out, you will resist new experiences and people. Familiarity becomes your friend. Comfortability turns into your constant companion. Sameness develops into your relationship safety net.

Oftentimes, individuals who get caught up in relationships that have them feeling like castaways have refused to listen to the warnings of close friends and family that the relationship may be headed for disaster. The longing for hoarding a castaway relationship is more important than reaching out to be saved from hurt and disaster. Nevertheless, they happily board a relationship journey that will ultimately find them shipwrecked on an island of despair and frustration.

Another bad love connection I experienced was with a man who was seventeen years my senior. I stayed sequestered on my personal *Gilligan's Island* for fear of having people voice their concerns about my unbalanced relationship. I did not want anyone to bust my bubble of the happy relationship that I convinced myself I was in. Since he gave me my own key to his place, I loved playing house with him. Planning dinner, cleaning up his apartment and planning our future together became my immediate and only focus during that time of my life. I truly was caught up in the rapture of love or so I thought.

But it was not all roses. During that time I would always have arguments with my mother, friends and anyone else who tried to warn me about this unhealthy relationship. His subtle hints for me to forsake everything I knew to be totally devoted to him 24/7 was eating away at other relationships I had. Because jealousy oozed from his pours anytime I showed others attention, I was always forced to divide my loyalty. I destroyed several longtime friendships because I totally neglected spending time with them, betrayed their trust and practically ignored them when I saw them out in public because I was embarrassed as to what they might think of him. I even ignored it when he told me he had been in jail for a crime that I am still not comfortable telling people about.

My whole life revolved around this dead-end relationship. I

thought this relationship was the best that I would ever get. I had little expectations for anything better. Without realizing it, the emotional ties that I had developed had a choke hold on me. My mind was so twisted by his dysfunctional affection and allegiance that I had sentenced myself to my own emotional prison. I was so far gone off of him that I was not trying to break loose regardless of what he did to me.

This bad relationship was like an uncontrollable forest fire. It destroyed every other relationship that was in my path. My life was in complete and utter shambles.

When this relationship was over (as it was destined to be), my rebuilding process was shameful and difficult. The people I had alienated were the same people that I turned to for comfort. Was it fair? No. It was indeed selfish of me. They had no obligation to try to rebuild any type of relationship with me. I happily took a one-year tour on a boat that was destined for disaster as soon as it pulled out of dock. So once my ship of love crashed, I needed the right people to rescue me and guide me back to civilization.

If you have a pattern of jumping into relationships haphazardly at maximum velocity in which you always isolate yourself from those who care about you, then you will end up a castaway on *Gilligan's Island.* You should never give a total stranger complete access to your life while shutting the door on the ones whom you have known for years. I challenge you to use wisdom, common sense and patience when meeting new people. Remember, even if they tell you their life story you still do not know them or what they are capable of. Only time reveals what people are really like.

The "Price Is Right"

Financial chaos can stress anyone out. Being stuck in a low paying job, the high cost of living, monumental debt, living from paycheck to paycheck or recovering from a divorce can have anyone wishing to find a pot of gold somewhere over the rainbow. Although statistics show that the number one cause for divorce is the issue of money, there are many relationship reruns that are entered into because of the love of money. One or both partners who have a deep desire to improve their financial portfolio rush the relationship for the almighty dollar.

Climbing the financial ladder of success is a natural dream that we all have at some point in our lives. However, when it is the primary factor for entering a relationship then the drive for success becomes unnatural. The "show me the money" mentality is one that can surface in individuals who have an unhealthy drive to jump to another financial bracket.

For example, April and Chester's dating situation was solely based on their love for money. April was a foster child who had five foster families within a span of thirteen years. Every family she was placed with seemed to struggle financially so April had to support herself when she was able to get a part-time job. When all of her friends in school got jobs for their weekend pleasures, April was working to support herself and pay some of the bills in the foster house. April grew up fast and learned the survival skills of hoarding everything she received because she never knew when she would have to pack up and leave.

April's hoarding skills filtered into her friendships as well as her dating relationships. Money and materialistic gain gave her feelings of social acceptance. She gravitated towards friends who were more financially secure than she was. Her charm seduced people into believing that she was loyal but in actuality she was strategizing her

38

plans as to how to get money out of them. Amongst her friends she frequently played the role of "Broke Betty" when the group planned outings. Of course they wanted April to go, so someone always assumed the financial responsibility for her.

April's only motive for finding a husband was so that she could have another stream of income to pay for her extravagancies she had longed for since she was a child. So in all of her dating relationships she was very aggressive, giving her companions ultimatums when the relationship seemed to be moving slowly or had little hopes of resulting in a marriage.

Chester, on the other hand, grew up in a family in which everything was handed to him on a silver platter. Although his family was not filthy rich they always had a lucrative flow of income. After his father was killed in the military, Chester's mother pampered her only son because she saw him as a replacement for her deceased husband. Chester was thirty-five years old and still lived with his mother. He was a job hopper but it did not matter because Chester had all access to his mother's banking accounts until his mother had to be admitted to a nursing home, which was around the same time that he met April.

Chester, who was between jobs when he met April, did not have to pay for anything when he and April went out the majority of the time. Because he was waiting to start a new job at a great factory that paid extremely well and had wonderful benefits, April willingly paid for all of the social activities that she and Chester participated in.

Chester immediately connected with April because of her willingness to assume total financial responsibilities of their dates as well as his living expenses until he received his first paycheck. She reminded him of his mother whom he dearly missed since she went to the nursing home. Chester and April became serious within a couple of months and he proposed to her on their sixth-month dating anniversary. They moved in together because they wanted to save money for the elaborate wedding that they were planning.

Two months after Chester and April moved in together, April was fired from her job. For the first time in his life, Chester was the primary income provider in a relationship. He was solely responsible for paying the mortgage until April found a job. Three months passed and April still had not found a job. Chester could not handle the pressure of someone depending on him for financial survival. Their relationship began to suffer due to the frequent fights, arguments and Chester's staying out all night.

April, who was only attracted to Chester after he told her about his new job, never made an emotional connection with Chester. She saw him as a means of financial gain which would eventually allow her to enter into a financial bracket that she longed to be in since her childhood. Chester, on the other hand, had never had to assume any financial responsibilities. When he met April, he was in desperate need of someone to take the place of his mother. When Chester was forced to be a grown up, it started to stress him out. He was no longer attracted to April and vice versa.

Because the relationship was not based on the solid foundations of trust, loyalty, love and commitment, it was inevitable that problems would arise when the finances were not flowing as intended. April and Chester found out the hard way that the price was not always right especially when one person looses their wheel of fortune.

You Have The "Wonder Woman/ Superman" Syndrome

The superhero complex that someone with supernatural powers will come in and rescue you from your troubles is another reason that most of us find ourselves in a relationship rerun. Superman and Wonder Woman are comic strip heroes brought to life in the movies and television. Every person they rescued was a part of a written script.

No one is going to hear their superhero theme song, change into a costume and rescue you from hardships. Please do not put that expectation on anyone. Avoid the fantasy that there is a person out there who has the power to save you because you will be disappointed every time.

You Are "The Young and the Restless"

Victor and Nikki Newman, Jack and Jill Abbott and Katherine Chancellor are characters in the imaginary world of Genoa City. The issues of love and life are not solved in an hour show. Frivolous decisions and lustful passion, often masquerading as love, have dreadful relationship consequences especially when you are young and restless.

A purpose-driven life can protect you from relationship restlessness. Co-author of the book, *Women's Journey to Wellness*, Michele Lanton points out, *"When we are not living in our purpose, we allow complacency to set in. This divergent pattern of approaching life can lead us on the journey of disharmony, ill-contentment and at times sheer unhappiness."* Operating in your purpose requires a tremendous amount of time, energy and focus. You tend to be so engulfed in discovering who you are and what you are suppose to be doing, that even the mere thought of settling for unwanted, unhealthy and unsatisfying relationships nauseates you.

You Think Your Relationship Is "As Good As It Gets"

Societal pressures are also a deciding factor in the huge dissatisfaction of couples who make hasty relationship choices. But what do you think will happen when you discover that God had something better for you than an "as good as it gets"? Or even worse, what will you do when your "as good as it gets" has turned into a nightmare on Elm Street?

When Bryant received his Masters degree in engineering, he was adamant about not succumbing to the social pressures of marrying his on-again-off-again (mostly off-again) college sweetheart of seven years, Sasha. Bryant and Sasha started dating as freshmen in college and remained serious throughout their college careers even though they attended separate schools 1,000 miles away from each other. Family, friends and even their foes knew that after Sasha graduated with her law degree, Bryant's fabulous graduation present would be an engagement ring that would make Bugs Bunny choke because of all of the carats it had.

However, Bryant and Sasha knew that their relationship was not ready for marriage. Even though they were not actively pursuing relationships with other people, both refused to adopt the "as good as it gets" philosophy in their relationship.

"I honestly love Bryant," Sasha confessed. "But deep down, both us knows in our hearts that he's not my husband nor am I his wife. We are in each others' lives as preparation for the next relationship."

Sasha and Bryant made a mature relationship decision not to marry each other or adopt the "as good as it gets" philosophy that their loved ones had regarding their relationship. Instead of planning their wedding, as every one had hoped, Sasha and Bryant were writing a relationship exit strategy. They knew that they would need to eventually embrace the idea that their relationship needed to end.

In conclusion, there is a thin line between love and hate so love connections should not be rushed into. Dishonesty, disregarding others emotions, hiding your authentic self and compromising your values all contribute to turning a happy love affair into a hateful exchange of emotions. Settle for nothing less than God's best when it comes to pursuing love connections. Being emotionally mature enough to differentiate the specific reasons and seasons for love connections is not only a sign that you are healthy but also whole enough to patiently wait to enjoy the right relationship with the right person at the right time.

REFLECTION EXERCISE
"REVEAL IT SO YOU CAN HEAL IT"

1. Describe in detail your worst dating relationship? Who was it with? What happened? How long did the drama last?

2. What signs of incompatibility did you ingore in the beginning of the relationship? Why did you ignore them?

Episode 2:
If It Isn't Love, Then What Is It?

"True love is unconditional, universal and unending."
—*Tanya White*

The bible says that "love is patient, love is kind. It does not envy, it does not boast, it is not proud. It is not rude, it is not self-seeking, it is not easily angered, it keeps no record of wrongs. Love does not delight in evil but rejoices with the truth. It always protects, always trusts, always hopes, always perseveres. Love never fails." (1 Corinthians 13:4-8). Sometimes what you think is love, unfortunately usually is a relationship of convenience that is temporarily tickling your surface level emotions instead of satisfying the inner parts of your soul. But if it isn't love, then what is it?

Many relationships of convenience quickly turn into emotional and mental poison. A poisonous relationship generally involves people who are:

Pessimistic a large majority of the time and seldom contribute to maturing the relationship.

Only seeing the other as a physical being, neglecting to nurture their emotional and spiritual side.

Insisting that all of the relationship problems are due to the other persons' faults, failures, family members, friends or focus on other things.

Spitting out ultimatums and demands to change the others' habits and hangout spots.

Openly degrades or argues with the other in public.

Needing continuous attention and affirmation to prove relationship loyalty and commitment.

Sadly, most people try to keep the details of their toxic love affairs on the down low as I confessed in the previous chapter. However, keeping a relationship secret is one thing that can kill you softly. In *The Secrets Men Keep*, Stephen Arterburn writes that *"because people are too ashamed to admit their flaws or failings to others they resort to stuffing secrets in a dark corner of their soul where they pick away at their self-image for a lifetime."* A host of people believe that relationship secrets are not harmful but a protective measure used to maintain peace in their lives. But on the contrary, secrets are infectious cancers which bring about perpetual turmoil.

Relationship secrets dredge up regret. But you can prevent relationship regret when you:

1. **Let go of living unhealthy external fantasies:** When you have unhealthy cravings to achieve happiness, you tend to rationalize your fantasies to fit your reality. Living unhealthy external fantasies is destined to cause you internal conflict.

2. **Listen to what people say:** If you let people talk long enough, they will tell you who they really are. When this happens decide if you can unconditionally accept the person. If you can not, then it would not be wise to spend your energies developing the relationship. Do not waste time fooling yourself.

3. **Look intently at what people do:** Actions speak louder than words. Watch what people do far more than what they say. Authentic attitudes are displayed in daily actions.

Mending the pieces of your life after a poisonous partnership requires immediate action. You will either need to remove yourself from the venomous environment, thoroughly cleanse the infected area or decontaminate your system entirely. In summary, it is best that you let the poisonous relationship go so that you can grow and flow.

Episode 3:
Happily Unhappy Days

"Happiness is not a final destination found in a person, place or thing. It is daily contentment found within yourself, by understanding what brings you an authentic pleasant experience of love, hope and peace without having feelings of shame or hiding your true self." —Tanya White

The conclusion of every book usually always ends with "And they lived happily ever after." But although happily ever after is oftentimes associated with fairy tales, it is possible for it to be a reality in your life. Everyone wants to be happy. Even the Queen of Hip/Hop Soul, Mary J. Blige desperately cried out "All I really want is to be happy." However, society has erroneously persuaded people into thinking that happiness is an easily attainable, independent and finite emotion entangled in the company of another person. This falsehood has driven millions of people to get trapped in what I call the *Happily Unhappy Syndrome.*

48

True happiness is a state of having the feelings of love, peace, pleasure, joy and a sense of authentic contentment. On the contrary, being happily unhappy is when you are masking your true desires in order to conform to people's expectations. You may shape activities, friendships, goals and moral ethics based on standards other than your own. Being happily unhappy is when your external smile hides your internal frown.

I spent many happily unhappy days in most of my dating relation-ships. No one forced me into this state. I was enslaved to the notion of living happily unhappy for the sake of having a companion in my life. There were several reasons why I chose to live in this miserable state. First, I refused to heal my hurts. It was much easier to self-medicate the hurt by entering into a lackluster relationship with someone. Ignoring my pain was less complicated. I did not want to face the excruciating pain of recovering from my past hurts because I would have to take an in-depth look at three important figures in my life: me, myself and I.

Secondly, I did not want to address conflicts that arose in my relationships. Not because I was afraid of conflict. But I was afraid of being rejected by my companion if the conflict was never resolved. I thought keeping the peace was less stressful than confronting the conflict. Finally, I frequently hid my true thoughts and personality because I had not yet discovered my authentic self. I would literally become the woman my boyfriend wanted me to be.

I gravitated towards lopsided dating relationships. I frequently made most of the efforts to spend time with the other person, planned all the outings and initiated the dates. It was no big deal for me to ac-cept behavior that was disrespectful and degrading from the men I was dating. I did not want to cause any problems that would make him angry. I put on a mask of satisfaction that was next to impossible to un-veil as I continued to stay stuck in the happily unhappy syndrome. No

49

matter how severe or dangerous the incompatibilities were, it took me forever to accept them. I did not care if the blatant signs of dysfunction were oozing out like hot lava on Mount St. Helens. I would choose to stay happily unhappy for one of three reasons:

1. I had invested too much of my time, money and talent in the relationship.
2. I wanted to flee the embarrassment of failing.
3. I was simply trapped into living a fantasy.

If you can identify with any of the above then you may be stuck in the happily unhappy syndrome. In *Relationships 101,* John Maxwell suggests, *"Possessing respect, shared experiences, trust, reciprocity and mutual enjoyment are essential for solid relationships."* Solid, long lasting and committed dating situations are seldom created from unhealthy compromise, ignoring the truth or avoiding conflict. Life is too short for you to short change yourself from experiencing authentic happiness by settling for unhappy companionships. Those types of relationships are primarily superficial and are successful for only a short time.

So how do you break the cycle of living happily unhappy? Terry McMillan recently explained in an interview on *Real Life Divas* that she is exploring the concept of true happiness in her next book project entitled *Getting Back To Happy.* Many people loose their zest for genuine happiness after a major life transition such as divorce, children leaving home, betrayal or tragedy. She continued to suggest that the only way that someone can truly find their way back to happiness is through reinventing their life.

After every disappointment and discouraging break up, instead of reinventing my life and learning the life lessons, I engaged in another string of unwanted, unsatisfying and unhealthy relationships. Because my confidence level was gradually disappearing, more dysfunctional relationship reruns followed. With my body language, subtle compromises of integrity and masking my true feelings, I was silently screaming, "Please define me. Tell me who I should be. I accept any and all applicants." Grabbing hold to whoever became my normality. I had no clear vision for my life. The Bible teaches that where there is no vision, people will perish and I was on the fast track to a life of self-destruction. I lacked vision plus I had low self-confidence.

Valorie Burton gives wonderful insight in her book, *Why Not You,* as to why people are not confident. She says that you tend to be less confident when you are:

▶ Not prepared

▶ Outside of God's will

▶ Pushing something to happen before it is time

▶ Making an emotional decision rather than a spiritually guided one

▶ Buying into lies or stereotypes that dissuade you

▶ Basing your confidence on superficialities

▶ Busy comparing yourself to others

▶ Setting an unachievable goal of perfection

▶ Setting a goal that you are not yet ready to achieve

▶ Not taking full responsibility for your actions

▶ Trying to do something that God does not mean for you to do because it is outside of your purpose, gifts, talents and passion

51

Sadly, I struggled with all of the above listed. It was inevitable that I would fall prey into a cycle of bad dating choices. To break the cycle I had to reinvent or redefine some critical areas of my life which impacted my dating selection. Examining the below nine areas is a preventative strategy against dating reruns. You must redefine your:

Hope—Do not allow your previous dating disappointments to contaminate your hope for attracting healthy and purposeful dating choices.

Attitude—Stinking thinking distorts your ability to make rational decisions. Begin to flood your atmosphere with positive thoughts and optimistic people so that your dating attitude will change. A changed attitude always changes action.

Purpose—Do you know why you are here? Do you know what you are supposed to be doing with your life? Discover your passion and talents then you will uncover your true purpose. A purpose driven life invites the right people in your circle.

Practices—Prepare a new strategy for meeting new people. If you keep doing what you have always done you can not help but to get what you have always gotten. Dare to do something different.

Integrity—A questionable character is a magnet for questionable characters that will eventually cause you to compromise your own character. Integrity in word and deed is a like Teflon coating. It makes you resistant to corrosion and insulates you from the harmful relationship pollutants.

Needs—Determine what your basic dating needs are emotionally, physically, spiritually, socially and financially for happiness. Failure to patiently wait for suitable candidates who can meet your needs lowers your relationship immune system which makes you prone to relationship disease.

Expectations—People treat us according to the expectations we have communicated to them. Expect little and that is exactly what you will receive.

Social circles—If your entire circle of friends and family includes people who are happily unhappy in their own dating or marriage relationships then it is next to impossible for you to have realistic models for authentic relationship happiness. You may need to do one of three things: disconnect some negative connections, reconnect some positive connections or find new connections in your circle of influence.

Self-confidence—Self-confidence is not arrogance. It is exuding a steadfast belief that you are fearfully and wonderfully made in the image of God. It is loving yourself the way God loves you—flaws and all.

Yes, true happiness can come to your life if you want it to. But it is your responsibility to decide whether you will actually live it or just lust after it. Once you are on the path of building your confidence, authentic happiness will be unleashed in your life. As a result, you will be allergic to the façade of the happily unhappy syndrome. The real you will start to shine through. Discover your authentic happiness so that you will begin to have the right people in your life.

REFLECTION EXERCISE
"BREAKING THE HAPPILY UNHAPPY SYNDROME"

Redefine your personal framework for happiness by answering the below questions:

1. Complete the statement "Happiness to me is..." Include the people, places and things that truly give you a pleasant experience of love, hope and peace without feelings of shame or negative compromise.

2. What steps must be taken in order for your life to resemble your definition of happiness?

3. What fears or obstacles will you have to overcome to pursue true happiness?

4. Does your relationship align with your new definition of happiness? If not, do you need to reposition, redefine or release this relationship?

Episode 4:
The Facts of Life:
You've Got the Wrong People in Your Life

"There is no such thing as neutral people.
They're either a help or a hindrance."
— Anonymous

W hen you become oblivious to setting dating boundaries, communicating your needs and establishing expectations the first time someone shows a smidgen of interest in you, you're wearing the emotional blindfolds. You will rush the relationship and allow the wrong people to become a fixture in your life. When you have emotional blindfolds you justify the wrong relationship choices by using statements such as:

"I know that I am doing wrong but I am happy."

"He/she is married, but they are getting a divorce so that we can be together."

"I can't control the way I feel. I need them in my life."

"We have nothing in common, but being with somebody is better than being by myself."

"Everybody is trying to prevent me from being happy. They just don't understand."

"Nobody's perfect. They will change eventually."

"They are going through a tough time. I can't leave them now."

"I am just helping them until they get on their feet."

"We moved in together to save money. We are going to get married anyway."

"I am not judging their past. Everybody has done something that they regret."

"People are just jealous of our relationship."

Intentionally ignoring relationship incompatibilities by putting on emotional blindfolds will take you on an unnecessary emotional rollercoaster filled with distractions, discouragements, depression or even danger in some cases. The below are just a few dreadful love connections who will have you lost in translation if you do not face the facts of life that they just may not be the right person for you.

The Hell Date

There is a reality show on Black Entertainment Television (BET) called *Hell Date*, which matches unsuspecting dating contestants with a potential candidate who, on the surface, seems to be the perfect partner. The hell dater, who is a paid actor or actress, masquerades as a compatible partner for the innocent victim. Eventually, during a series of three dates, the potential candidate becomes increasingly irritating turning what was supposed to be a match made in heaven, into the date straight from the inner courts of hell.

Most of the hell daters demonstrate annoying and intolerable behavior on the first date. Meanwhile, the alarms of relationship incompatibility continue to ring louder and louder as they progress to the next date. However, the contestant willingly endures the craziness for several reasons:

▶ People are watching them, documenting their event and they want to appear that everything is okay to shun embarrassment.

▶ They are hoping to receive a little glimmer of hope through patience and compromise that everything will work out for the best.

▶ They are wanting a free meal or to participate in other activities that were planned on the date.

The *Hell Date* reality show unfortunately is a dismal depiction of how most relationship reruns begin. Please do not pursue a relationship with a hell dater. Behavior that is suspicious, disturbing or demented in the beginning of a relationship only grows as you invest additional time and energy. A hell date is always a prelude to a hellish relationship. So pay attention to the warning signs.

The Incredible Hulk

Bill Bixby made this series a Friday night hit show between 1977 and 1982. Dr. David Banner was a research scientist who was exposed to an extreme amount of radiation during an experiment. After the traumatic accident, whenever someone taunted him or attacked him, he would loose his temper and would transform into the insanely strong seven-foot green-eyed monster called the Incredible Hulk. The Incredible Hulk would usually hurt those who threatened him. When his fits of rage were over, the Incredible Hulk would flee the scene and go to a place to cool down. During the cool down period, the hulk would return to his calmer personality of Dr. David Banner.

Maybe you have dated or are dating the Incredible Hulk or the Incredible Hulktress. You frequently walk on egg shells to avoid experiencing the potential volatile bouts of anger. But, at the same time, you welcome him or her back with open and empathetic arms following each explosive occurrence hoping that this will be the last time that they will flip out.

If a person shows signs that they are unable to effectively manage their anger then there is absolutely nothing you can do to save them. You can not love them into not being angry. Talking them out of their episodes of rage is ineffective. People who exhibit fits of rage like the Incredible Hulk need professional help to work through their anger issues. It is not your job to save them. Your job is to save yourself from unnecessary and potentially dangerous dating situations.

Bad Boys

Every woman wants a bad boy, right? Well, that is what everyone says. I used to be very much attracted to the bad boys—the gangsters—the thugalicious type. Whew! I held strong to the Mc Lyte philosophy: I had to get a rough neck!

In my experience bad boys are loads of fun, brutally honest and unashamedly authentic. They are focused on getting exactly what they want and make no apologies. Bad boys are go-getters, protective and always on the grind to get the dollar, dollar bill so that they can provide for their family. All of these magnetic qualities are what most women desire in every man. But it becomes a disastrous recipe for love when illegal, unethical and immoral means are used. Bad boys will always get you mixed up in some very bad trouble.

Naughty Girls

What man would not welcome the chance to be involved with a naughty girl? A girl who is sexually liberated and willing to fulfill every manly desire. A lady who will have every man she is with floating on cloud nine without pressuring them to be in a committed relationship. She knows what she wants and has mastered how to get it.

A majority of the men I asked said that they would love to have a naughty girl for the reasons that I stated above. But that is hogwash. Generally, men who are with naughty girls can not handle the sexual openness of the relationship. Issues such as jealousy, feelings of rejection and abandonment stir up a flame that becomes a four alarm fire in this love connection.

The Cheater

What's Done In The Dark is not just a title of Tyler Perry's hit stage play but a universal fact of life. Yet, most people who cheat believe that their secret escapades and infidelities are immune to this philosophy. Secrets and lies have a way of catching up with you no matter how secure you think your plan is executed. Someone who cheats usually is frequently caught in lies or inconsistencies.

Just in case you have an intuition that your significant other is cheating, whether it is emotional or physical, below are some clear-cut warning signs of infidelity. For a detailed list of the warning signs, and other information about relationship infidelity, please visit www. truthaboutdeception.com.

▶   Unaccounted for birth control
▶   Missing clothing

- Unexplainable or unaccounted for loss of time
- Drastic changes in sex drive (can either be too eager or not interested at all)
- Emotional and physical disengagement
- Excessive time away from home usually using the excuse of working or other community involvements
- Very critical, hostile or abusive
- Always picking arguments and blaming you for what you are not doing in the relationship
- Frequent threats of leaving or finding someone better
- Unwilling to make firm future commitments
- Blames the other persons' family, friends, personal habits or physical appearance for relationship unhappiness or dissatisfaction.

Unfortunately, most of the time cheaters have ripped away at their companions' self-esteem and confidence. Their inappropriate behavior becomes acceptable and expected. Instead of confronting the cheater, the cheatee tries to "make things right" hoping that the person will stop cheating and make a full commitment to fidelity.

There is nothing that you can magically do to make a person stop cheating. Therefore, you must decide if you will continue accepting the degradation from the cheater's actions or realize that you deserve honesty, respect, truth and fidelity from your significant other. The choice is yours but I pray that you decide the latter.

The One Under Deep Cover

Laurence Fishburne played narcotics detective Russell Stevens, Jr., in the movie *Deep Cover.* In a big undercover case, Fishburne's character had to pose as a drug dealer in order to arrest a drug lord. Because he was so good at playing the role he was told to play, Fishburne swiftly advanced to the top of the drug chain and gained the trust of the key dealers who had power, money and influence. Throughout the entire process, the undercover world was so sinister and seductive to him that Fishburne's character lost his true identity.

Have you ever discovered that the person you were dating was not who they portrayed themselves to be? They talked the part. They even looked the part. They even surrounded themselves with the right social circles to add validity to their undercover persona. Yet in actuality they were on the down low either sexually, emotionally, financially, spiritually or professionally.

Sadly, we live in a society that celebrates people wearing masks. It's considered socially acceptable to become a poser instead of being the real thing. Deep feelings of betrayal and distrust will surface when you are involved with someone who is pretending to be someone else. As the lies start mounting up like a heap of cow manure, disconnect this love connection. Save yourself the emotional clean up that will occur as a result of the secrets you will discover from this undercover lover.

Fatal Attractions

I believe every man in America was scared out of their bridges when they watched the 1987 thriller *Fatal Attraction*. This frightening realistic saga masterfully shows the consequences of what happens when you enter a sexual relationship with someone you hardly know because your hormones are jumping insatiably, especially when you are married to someone. All men and women should seriously observe the below personality traits of a potential fatal attraction as stated on www.womensaccount.com.

Rough Treatment

This common behavior entails grabbing of the arms, kicking, shoving, pulling hair or slapping. It can also lead to forced sexual intercourse on occasions.

Quick Shallow Attachments and Intimate Verbal Expression

Saying "I love you," making unrealistic promises, introduction to important family, friends or sexual intercourse within the first few dates blind you to this fatal attraction. They frequently bring up the topic of cohabitation or marriage soon after the first date. If you have unresolved issues of rejection, abandonment or have abusive relationship reruns you will tend to thrive off this fatal attraction convincing yourself that the relationship is healthy and will last forever.

Frightening Temper

Bouts of rage, frequent fights with others, blaming others' actions for the angry outburst should be expected. You will become fearful and ignore discussing the problem to avoid their anger being directed towards you.

Kills Your Confidence

Using verbal arguments or repeated put downs is a harmful strategy that fatal attractions use to suck away your confidence. They also question every decision you make. They challenge you when you disagree with them usually bringing your loyalty into question. Statements such as "If you really loved me you would do this" are spouted out several times a day. You begin to walk on eggshells in public and private, battling feelings of low self-esteem and shame because you desperately want to leave but are unable to muster up the strength to do so.

Forces You Into Isolation or Cutting Off Your Social Support

System

They are usually afraid that someone close to you will expose them. As a result, fatal attractions subtly try to encourage you to rid your life of everyone close to you who has the voice of rationality. They want to have total control over you. Accusations such as "Everyone is against our relationship," "People are jealous of our love," "Your friend made a pass at me" are also strategies of isolation in this destructive relationship choice.

Have No Outside Interest Other Than You

Fatal attractions are very codependent. They usually have few friends, a low motivation for personal success, very few activities independent of the relationship and demand your undivided attention. They nag you about friends, activities and aspirations because it takes your focus off the relationship.

Nothing is Ever Enough or Every Problem is Your Fault

Blame is prevalent in this relationship. They will spend hours, days, even weeks dredging up the same issue to argue about so that you will eventually feel guilty.

Tries to Convince You That Your Friends and Family Do Not Like Them

Because those close to you will notice the negative change in your personality and the added stress that this draining relationship brings to you, the mere mention of any family or friends ignites a heated debate. They will argue with your family or friends they feel threatened by while forcing you to side with them. You will avoid talking to those who care for you when your fatal attraction is around or cut others off completely.

Sense of Entitlement

Whether it is having complete access to your money, home or car, an unstable attraction will impose subtle demands on your personal property. They will give you access to all their personal property such as keys to their home, car or codes to bank accounts and expect you to do the same. They will make you feel guilty or say that you are selfish when you refuse to comply. Fatal attractions pressure you to merge your money, property and accounts with theirs because they will always come out ahead financially in the deal.

The Breakup Panic

Whenever they fear that you will break up with them, then expect the river of tears to flow, loads of promises to change or even an increased amount of passionate sexual advances to be used as a diversion tactic. They will also stalk you, call excessively and drop by your house, work or party unannounced when you have expressed in interest to break up with them.

Excessive Threats to Kill Themselves or You

Threats of suicide or homicide from a fatal attraction may be used as a strategy to keep you bound to the relationship. They make insinuations such as "No one will miss me when I am gone" or "I will kill you before I let you leave me" routine. Please do not brush these threats off as your companion's ploys for attention. Suicidal and homicidal threats are no light matter. If all the other signs do not snap you back into reality then the homicidal and suicidal thoughts should encourage you to cut this relationship loose.

I did not need www.womensaccount.com to give me a list of the signs of a fatal attraction. The relationship I mentioned earlier in the *Gilligan's Island* section was my fatal attraction experience. Although it was not a physical fatal attraction, my bad decision to pursue a relationship with Lloyd had me emotionally lifeless, professionally stagnant and socially isolated. Because at that time my esteem was virtually bankrupt and my craving for companionship was in overdrive, I quickly invested in this fatal attraction on all relationship levels: sexually, emotionally, socially and financially. I was dangerously in love or better yet, dangerously in lust.

After numerous therapy sessions, years of mending the other family relationships and friendships that I tarnished because of my distorted allegiance to Lloyd now I can automatically detect the signs when a Lloyd-like person is in my midst. But unfortunately, there is nothing anyone can do to persuade a person to leave a fatal attraction dating situation. Until a person wants to be free from a fatal attraction, they will stay bound to trying to make something out of nothing. Relationships with fatal attractions will have you sacrificing everything, even your life in many cases. Rushing to satisfy your desire for a love connection just may be the mind blowing decision that causes a fatal relationship collision.

Episode 5:
7 Reasons Why You Keep Crashing Into Relationship Reruns

"People approach you based on the level of integrity that they sense coming from you." —Bishop Joseph Walker, Nashville, TN, from the series "Play Time Is Over"

One summer, while driving to an afternoon picnic with some friends, I encountered an unexpected situation that created some added stress in my life. The sun was beaming, the weather was incredible and I was looking marvelous, if I say so myself. As I was sitting at the stop light listening to some peppy tunes on my stereo, I was terribly excited about having some much needed fun and relaxation with my friends. And then suddenly...SCREECH! BAM! CRASH! BOOM!

Out of no where I became an innocent victim of a three car wreck. Two cars, both racing to beat the yellow light, crashed into one another and eventually hit my car. What I thought was going to be a pleasant fun-filled day quickly turned into an afternoon of unplanned debris cleanup

66

because someone else was driving recklessly and irresponsibly.

When you are reckless about your dating decisions, you will also crash into a relationship reruns. There are seven ways in which you exhibit irresponsible behavior when pursuing love connections:

1. **Misrepresentation:** Not authentically being who you have been promoting yourself to be quickly dismantles trust and ultimately destroys relationships. Escape the temptation to transform yourself to meet other people's expectations. Be the unique fabulous person that God created you to be!

2. **Mouths:** What you say has an everlasting affect on people. Benjamin Franklin quoted, *"Remember not only to say the right thing in the right place. But far more difficult still is to leave unsaid the wrong thing at the tempting moment."* When you are angry, refuse to spit out words that you will regret later. Drama-proof your relationships by watching your mouth.

3. **Moods:** Avoid having frequent mood swings. Check your negative attitudes and uncontrollable moods. You can take people on a terrifying emotional roller coaster when you are moody all of the time.

4. **Misplaced Anger:** Acknowledge the root cause of your anger. Stop lashing out at innocent people. When you find yourself on edge it is probably best that you confront truth and find positive ways to release your negative energy.

5. **Misconceptions:** Ignoring conflicts start to play tricks on your mind. You begin to blow things out of proportion and develop misconceptions concerning your relationship. You will become

paranoid about anyone and everything. Get to the bottom of the conflict immediately when it arises.

6. **Miscommunication**: It is completely unfair to assume that people can accurately read your mind, actions or secret codes. Ask questions when you have apprehensions or receive mixed messages. Also, when your partner asks why you are angry tell the truth. Say what you mean and mean what you say.

7. **Manipulation and Mischievous Actions**: If you are a controlling person then you will most likely engage in manipulative and mischievous acts whether you know it or not. These acts can be exhibited in many forms such as holding grudges, playing the victim role, ignoring people, withholding affection or forming replacement relationships with others solely based on unaddressed issues in another relationship. Be careful how you respond when things do not go your way.

Wrecked relationships can linger and create a heap of emotional debris. Avoid letting days, weeks, months, even years pass by before addressing problems in your relationships. If the relationship debris is not cleaned up then you will find yourself being cynical, closed off from new relationships or replacing troubled relationships with a relationship rerun.

REFLECTION EXERCISE
"CLEANING UP YOUR RELATIONSHIP DEBRIS"

1. From the actions listed in the chapter, identify the ones that contributed to your last wrecked relationship.

2. Do the actions stated in #1 still prohibit you from having healthy relationships? If so, explain why. Be very specific. (For example, if you have a fear of abandonment which prompts you to misrepresent yourself because you fear that people will not like the real you, then explore deep into your emotional wounds the where, when and how this fear took root in your life).

3. What steps will you take to heal from the hurt listed in #2? By what date will you begin implementing these steps?

Episode 6:
The Real Issues Behind Your Commitment Issues

"Love yourself first and everything else falls into line."
—Lucille Ball

Most people confess that they struggle with commitment phobia. Commitment is defined as being steadfast, serious minded or binding yourself to a particular course of action. Yet, everybody routinely becomes committed to a job, family, social circle or a business venture. Sometimes the commitment phobia excuse may be a cover up for a deeper issue. The real issue behind many commitment issues is more than likely rooted in fear.

Dr. Phil McGraw reports in his book, *Love Smart,* that, *"Some experts estimate that 80% of all choices are motivated by fear. It changes perception, behavior, your reactivity and it changes you into a state of paranoid self-preservation that will contaminate any relationship you get into."* Fear is a natural emotion that is a survival mechanism to protect us against danger. Fear is a response caused by the expectation of pain or danger. However, it becomes unnatural when it completely paralyzes you or prevents you from pursuing positive opportunities in your life. An unnatural fear can transform into paranoia, distrust, self sabotaging behaviors. This type of fear motivates you to make irrational dating decisions.

In a random survey I conducted I asked men and women from various backgrounds to list three fears that prohibit them from pursuing their optimal levels of success in the areas of family, spirituality, finances and intimate relationships. Below are the fears from the survey responses given in order from the greatest to the least:

▶ Fear of abandonment
▶ Fear of being alone
▶ Fear of change
▶ Fear of compromise
▶ Fear of failure
▶ Fear of hard work
▶ Fear of being happy
▶ Fear of increased responsibility
▶ Fear of loosing relationships
▶ Fear of repeating past relationship failures
▶ Fear of rejection
▶ Fear of success
▶ Fear of being vulnerable
▶ Fear of what others think and say
▶ Fear of knowing and confronting the reality of the truth

In addition to fear, other reasons were doubt and low self-esteem. While these are legitimate emotions, it is imperative that you take the necessary steps to overcome these fears if you genuinely hope to have healthy and satisfying relationships. Moreover, continuously ignoring your fears will birth a sense of desperation. Desperation can be described as a reckless or dangerous form of despair. Generally, you have anxious cravings or risk everything on dating relationships that are dangerous or have serious consequences when you are desperate.

Most people in relationship reruns will deny that they are desperate. They will mask their foolish risk taking as satisfying a basic human desire for companionship. When the relationship fails, their mantra becomes the "It is better to have love and lost than to have never loved at all" philosophy instead of admitting that they were desperate. Desperate people who make such rash decisions will soon find themselves suspended between sanity and insanity.

Episode 7:
Something Just Ain't Right

"When people show you who they really are, believe them."
—Dr. Maya Angelou

There are many times, at the beginning stages of a dating relationship, that you will have what I call a Keith Sweat moment of enlightenment. You will have intuitions that something just ain't right with your relationship. Yet, in efforts to avoid being stuck on what author Ian Kerner calls "the dating treadmill," you ignore your instinct. Hopes that with a little hard work, undenying love and self-determination, you pray that whatever is not right about the relationship will magically become right.

The worst masquerade that you can ever perpetuate is making excuses for the wrong in search of your Mr. or Mrs. Right. Still, even if you refuse to acknowledge the warning signs, they are still grossly apparent for you and those around you to see.

If the person you are contemplating giving your mind, body and time to exhibits one or all of the below signs, on a consistent basis, then put the brakes on the relationship before you get too deep into a situation that takes you years to climb out of. Take heed to the below 8 behavior patterns that will always warn you that something just ain't right.

1. **Drama**

   "And the Oscar goes to." A person who thrives off creating theatrical and crazy episodes every time things are not the way they expect will drain you mentally and physically. Contrary to popular opinion, relationships do not have to be induced with a daily dose of high impact drama. Peace can become a constant factor in your relationship.

2. **Distance**

   This person usually has some trust issues that has not been resolved. They may also be hiding something or someone which will question their integrity, honesty and loyalty. Or, they may not be truly ready to commit to the time and emotional energy that it requires to be in a healthy and satisfying relationship. Instead of communicating their true feelings, they become distant and aloof. It will become impossible to make an authentic love connection with someone who distances themselves from you emotionally or physically.

3. **Disappearing Acts**

   Inability to handle conflict, correctly and calmly, is usually the motive behind someone who physically disappears without a trace and then pops back into your life as though nothing has happened. Running away is never healthy because eventually whatever you are trying to escape from is always there when you get back. Feelings of insecurity, doubt and emotional immaturity are the fundamental deficiencies of someone who is always fleeing the scene. You can count on issuing a relationship APB (All Points Bulletin) for this partner who is always AWOL (Absent Without Leave).

4. **Decreased Dependability**

"I'll call you tomorrow." Men, seven whole days may have passed and she still has not called you. "Yeah, I will fix that for you." Girlfriend, six months later, you still may be waiting for him to make good on his promise. If you cannot depend on someone for the little things, then when it comes to the big things in the relationship, what makes you think that the person will be there for you? Observe how reliable a person is especially in your times of need. You will always wind up waiting for a person who is an emotional, financial and physical "no-show" when you accept the behavior from this love connection.

5. **Doubting Your Loyalty**

A person who frequently doubts your loyalty begins every conversation with statements such as "If you really loved me" and ends them with a challenge for you to prove your loyalty. I call this an emotional and mental "one-night stand." Much like someone trapped in the adrenaline rush of engaging in a number of emotionless sexual encounters, the pressure to prove your loyalty eventually leaves you feeling used and abused. Subsequently, the person making the demands does not draw closer to you once you have passed the challenge but moves further away. They are motivated by being in complete emotional control. It becomes a relationship game of "Simon Says."

6. Desperation

Anxiousness, ultimatums, the urgency to engage in a sexual relationship and marriage commitment are just a few symptoms of someone who is desperate for a love connection. Control becomes the usual strategy when someone is desperate. Desperate people bring division, discouragement and doubt into the relationship ultimately making the union deplorable.

7. Distraction From Important Life Priorities And Goals

When a person wants you to give up the things that are most important to you for the sake of building a relationship, then they are not respecting you as a person or the goals that you had before you met them. This type of person usually does not have any goals for themselves. They are not confident in their abilities to succeed. They become secretly envious of your life goals so they distract you from yours.

8. Deceitful Acts

Trust will always be an issue with someone who willfully and intentionally engages in deceitful habits. Issues such as infidelity, betrayal, manipulation, theft, strife, moral and spiritual compromise will slowly strip you of your confidence and self-esteem if you choose to ignore this unhealthy relationship sign. Stop excusing other people's excuses for their negative actions.

All of us have an innate survival instinct to know when we are not in an emotionally safe dating situation. When you have a feeling that something is not right in your relationship then it probably is not.

Episode 8:
Dating Down Does Not Keep You Lifted Up

"When it comes to dating, some people settle down, some people settle for whoever and whatever and some people refuse to settle for anything less than what truly makes them happy."
—Carrie Bradshaw (Sarah Jessica Parker), Sex and the City

"I always date down. It keeps my self-esteem high," Patrice confessed.

"What do you mean date down?" I inquired.

"Dating down is deliberately dating someone who has less than you do financially, intellectually, professionally, socially and emotionally so that they can think that they have hit the jackpot and smother you with loads of attention. It makes me feel a little superior to them so I am in complete control of the relationship. Feeling superior in my dating relationships lifts my self-esteem. I need for men to be totally into me and to think that I am the best thing that has happened to them.

Girl, I need a lot of attention from men that is why I date down."

"Patrice that is not healthy," I said in shock. "Feeling superior to someone does not help keep your self-esteem lifted."

"It may not over a long period of time, but it works for a while," Patrice boldly added.

"Dating down. Do women really do that?" I continued to ask.

"It's not just women," Gerald interrupted. "Men date down too. I do it from time to time myself when my confidence is crashing."

"Wow!"

This was the topic of conversation at breakfast one Saturday morning with a group of friends who I fellowship with frequently to discuss family, finances and romance. The subject of dating down literally floored me. I could not grasp the concept of "dating down." It threw me for a loop. I could not internalize why such beautiful and financially independent professional men and women confessed that they engaged in a dysfunctional dating cycle to help keep their self-esteem high.

But a small inner voice reminded me that this was not a concept that was foreign to me. I may not have called it "dating down." However, I had on many occasions subconsciously gravitated towards men whom I had absolutely nothing in common with. In fact, the men in those "dating down" relationships gave me tons of uninterrupted attention, seemed more dedicated to making sure that I was totally satisfied and did not hesitate engaging frequently in excessive amounts of public displays of affection. But, like oil and water, these relationships did not mix.

A vast number of people who lower their standards believe that they can change a person into whoever they want them to be. If the person does not meet your dating standards and expectations when you first meet them then you should not force the relationship. Dating them, giving them money, taking them places that they have never been before, moving them into your house and the other crazy antics will never satisfy you because in the deep chambers of your soul, you know that you have settled for less than what you deserve.

This concept of "dating down" is the premise for Ian Kerner, Ph.D., national best-selling book *Be Honest—You're Not That Into Him Either.* Kerner argues that today's daters, particularly women, are injecting themselves with intentional dating misery because they've gotten stuck on the dating treadmill or force themselves into relationships that go-nowhere. Kerner writes, *"Go on enough bad dates and your hopes of finding love are sure to diminish. You start to make adjustments, taking the realistic and pragmatic approach. You begin to settle. You know that frogs don't turn into princes, so you lower your standards enough until it gets difficult to tell the two apart."* In essence, this is the reasoning for Patrice and Gerald's "dating down" concept. Dating someone to build up your self-esteem is ineffective. The key to self-esteem is developing a love for oneself.

Compatibility must be present on all levels—spiritually, financially, emotionally, professionally and intellectually—for any dating relationship to have longevity. Compatibility does not mean an exact sameness. However, it does mean that both of you are on the same playing field. But when you get caught up in the fantasy that "dating down" is your only hope for romance then your relationship becomes like a hamster running on the wheel. It runs around in a fast circle without a definite destination.

Episode 9:
R-E-S-T: The 20 Keys To Healthy Love Connections

"Like nicotine and reality TV watching, "in the meantime" dating can be habit forming. And eventually become an addiction of sorts. More important, you may convince yourself there's something real between you just to avoid the fact that you've been exerting so much energy for something that doesn't count." —Ian Kerner, Ph.D., *Be Honest—You're Not That Into Him Either: Raise Your Standards and Reach For The Love You Deserve*

No more drama" was the wise advice that the Queen of Hip Hop Soul, Mary J. Blige gave to the world in 2002. Yet despite the peace that comes as a result of abiding by a *no more drama* philosophy, many individuals live the opposite when it comes to dating relationships. Sadly, many individuals surround themselves with chaotic, morally compromising and drama induced relationships.

I had the awesome opportunity to interview Bern Nadette Stanis also know as "Thelma" of the 1970's hit show *Good Times,* to discuss why there is so much drama plaguing many dating relationships today, which is also the theme of her new book *Situations 101.* Ms. Stanis shared some wise insights to the dating dilemma that is prohibiting many healthy relationships. Read what she had to share about choosing healthy dating situations. To read the entire interview, please browse the newsletter archive section on my website at www.tanyawhite.com.

TANYA: Why is it so difficult for people to maintain healthy dating relationships?

BERN NADETTE: The dating format has changed. Years ago there were certain standards that were followed. For example, women allowed men to chase them and men had to meet the woman's parents to receive the okay for them to date or court as it was called. But today people follow their own standards. Women do not let men chase them. No one ever meets each other's family before a relationship is pursued. There is the mentality that whatever works for me is okay. Everything is a free-for-all, wild mixture of personal rules which only lead to chaos and brokenness.

TANYA: What are 3 essentials to forming healthy dating relationships?

BERN NADETTE: Honoring one another, respecting what people want and refusing to get caught up in living in a "make believe" marriage. A "make believe" marriage is when people have become emotionally tied to the relationship too soon without taking the time to learn about one another. When it comes to dating choices, people cannot panic when they desire to have a relationship because they will start grabbing at anyone without learning who the person really is. So by the time they learn that the person may have a temper, has commitment problems or other issues that make them incompatible, they are so caught up in the "make believe" marriage that they have to work backwards in building the relationship.

TANYA: Explain how dating the wrong person creates unnecessary drama in your life and ultimately prevents you from maximizing your purpose?

BERN NADETTE: In any relationship we must know what habits we can tolerate from others and what the relationship deal breakers are. For example, you may be attracted to someone because of how they look but then they gain weight. You can live with the weight gain because they are a nice person. But deal breakers are those things that you can not accept because it hurts your spirit and soul. When you compromise your deal breakers to be in a relationship with a person, you will eventually start to give them ultimatums. Ultimatums are a form of control. If you have to give people ultimatums then you should not be dating them anyway.

TANYA: Any final advice on how to have healthy and satisfying dating relationships?

BERN NADETTE: Date someone who you truly like and who wants the best for you and vice versa. Do not rush any relationship for the sake of being in a relationship. Be patient and take the time to learn all about the person to see if you like them. Love will come if you genuinely like the person you are dating.

This interview was confirmation that it is very attainable to be involved in a healthy, drama-free, loving and productive dating situation when you are not blinded by issues discussed in the previous episodes. I have concluded that there are 20 keys to having healthy love connections. Similar to the four stages that must occur in order for you to have a restful sleep, the four stages of relationship "R-E-S-T" should be evident in order to avoid falling into an unhealthy dating rerun.

STAGE I

The beginning stages of building healthy and satisfying love connections should involve an observation period. Before progressing to Stage II, the below traits need to be exhibited on the onset in both the group environment and one-on-one settings. For validity and consistency, I suggest that you observe these traits for about 1 to 3 months.

▸ **Respect**—Respect can be defined as honest appreciation and courtesy shown towards someone. Respect is an action and attitude shown towards you and others.

▸ **Effort**—Before any relationship can be on the path to success, both parties must be willing to put forth the effort. A healthy relationship can never be a one person show.

▸ **Self-aware**—Self-awareness is something that can not be manufactured. Someone who is self-aware is in touch with their authentic self, understands their strengths and is actively working on the areas of improvement. They accept responsibility for their failures and mistakes. Listening carefully to what people say concerning themselves is an initial indicator of the degree of self-awareness they exhibit.

▸ **Truth**—There is no such thing as little lies and big lies. A lie is a lie. Without truth, trust is absent in the relationship.

STAGE II

After about 3 months or more, usually a couple's occasional dates have turned into scheduled weekly activities. In addition to the "R-E-S-T" factors mentioned in Stage I, the below should be apparent if you decide to take the relationship to the next phase.

▶ **Realness**—Trying to be someone other than yourself is more difficult than being the real you. Failure to bring realness to the relationship creates distrust, distance and division between the two partners.

▶ **Easy-going**—To be easy-going is not to allow anything to happen without reacting. It means that you are relaxed, peaceful and respond calmly in agitated situations. Someone who frequently exhibits anxious, demanding or rigid behavior when you first meet them is more than likely to add more stress to the relationship as it grows.

▶ **Secure**—Insecure people doubt their partner's motives, loyalty and commitment level. A secure person feels confident in who they are, has assurance in their capabilities and exudes a healthy self perception. Pursuing a relationship with a secure person will greatly decrease unnecessary relationship drama.

▶ **Trustworthy**—From showing up for a scheduled date to following through on a promise, a trustworthy companion helps to create a peaceful, purposeful and productive relationship.

STAGE III

During this stage, peoples' true colors start shining through because you have known each other for at least 6 months or more. More than likely, introduction to each other's intimate friends and family has occurred and you have observed them in various settings. Consequently, if character inconsistencies are too excessive at this stage please do not ignore them.

▶ **Rational**—Irrational people create unwanted drama. Clear-headed, reasonable and sober-minded choices can be the difference between relationship turmoil and tranquility.

▶ **Ethical**—Ethical behavior is whatever is correct, upright and fair, both universally and personally. If this cannot be demonstrated throughout a person's daily actions, it certainly will not be a part of the relationship.

▶ **Significant**—If both parties have not become better people by being in the relationship, then the purpose of the relationship has been unproductive. Love connections should be more than social fun. The quality of conversation, emotional connection and time spent in the relationship should improve each person holistically. Healthy relationships should add another dimension of significance to the lives of both parties.

▶ **Tenderness**—A little tenderness can be the medicine that your companion needs when weariness, discouragement and failure spring up in their lives. However, showing tenderness does not mean that you camouflage truth. It means that you empathize, using wisdom to know when the timing is right to speak the truth in love.

STAGE IV

The rubber meets the road during this phase. Couples usually have been exclusively dating for a year or more. At this stage, the relationship should be progressing to another level of intimacy and lasting commitment such as marriage. Commonly, couples are weighing the pros and cons of the success and longevity of the relationship. Sensitive personal issues such as sickness, job trouble, family tragedy and other incidents have probably transpired. Please watch how your partner reacts to these issues. Also, be cognizant as to whether your companion draws closer to you emotionally or distance themselves during these troubling times.

▶ **Reciprocity**—Reciprocity is an equal exchange or willingness of support emotionally, physically, spiritually, financially and socially. Any imbalance stifles authentic and lasting relationship growth.

▶ **Encouragement**—Consistent encouragement fosters a supportive, inspirational and prosperous relationship. Not only will your partner persevere during tough times in the relationship, but also amidst hardships in their individual lives.

▶ **Steadfastness**—Steadfastness is the capability of not fleeing or avoiding the pressure when problems arise. Having the staying power to work through and eventually overcome trouble is valuable to wholesome relationships.

▶ **Transparent**—Being transparent clears up any obscurities or unanswered questions. It also develops a deeper level of emotional intimacy because vulnerabilities are shown. Inability to be transparent at this stage may be problematic, can foster unnecessary tension and ultimately make the relationship stagnant.

Many issues should be considered before deciding to connect with someone for lasting companionship or marriage. Love connections are so much more than two people having fun. They are more than having a person to fill your idle time. Dating relationships are important decisions concerning emotional partnerships that will either progress or postpone your ultimate life purpose. Be wise and patient because the right love connection will come at the right time.

REFLECTION EXERCISE
"DATING DEALMAKERS VS. DEALBREAKERS"

1. Define a healthy dating relationship according to your spiritual, emotional, professional and mental standards.

2. What values must a potential dating candidate possess in order for you to be compatible with them?

3. List your dating boundaries—physically, emotionally, spiritually and sexually. For each boundary list a consequence that you will impose if your date oversteps boundaries after you have clearly communicated them.

4. List 5 positive qualities that you bring to a dating relationship

5. Identify 3 issues that may hinder the success of your dating relationships. What are you currently doing to address these issues before you enter dating relationships?

6. Identify 5 dating deal breakers.

Series 2:
Friends—How Many Of Us Have Them?

"Friendships are maintained by similar attitudes, values, sensibility, affection and satisfying communication."
— Florence Isaacs, Toxic Friends, True Friends

*F*riends—How many of us have them? In 1984, Jalil, Ecstasy and Grandmaster Dee, who made up the powerful pioneer rap group Whodini, prompted us to take an honest look at the friendships in our lives. As the song suggests, sometimes we make the grave mistake of crowning people with the title of friend too loosely. A friend is someone who is more than a person with whom you share frequent fellowship. A friend is someone who is genuine, honest, faithful, trustworthy, forgiving, loyal and truthful during the best and worst times of your life.

Dr. Robin L. Smith wrote in a 2006 article via www.oprah. com, that *"A friend is someone who loves and supports you, who tells you the truth and is also willing to listen to the truth. A true*

90

friend is someone who brings out the best in you." Unfortunately, I have invested a tremendous amount of time and emotional energy crowning people with the title of friend who never earned the position.

I mistook uplifting conversation for unquestionable commitment. I seldom had a discussion with people to define friendship expectations, boundaries or compare values and beliefs. Varying differences in dealing with conflict, expressing the truth and having a clear definition of friendship, eventually strained the relationship. Discussing the foundations of friendship in the beginning, understanding the category of friendship, observing the level of reciprocity and paying close attention to how your friends respond to you in the presence of others will help you avoid foolish and frustrating friendships.

Episode 10:
What About Your Friends?

"It is best to pick your close friends who align with your same values and beliefs. Consciously design a close circle of friends who will support your life and all that you do and dream of doing."
—Jennifer Blair, Founder of Excavive Life Coaching

Research has proven that healthy friendships, even more so than love connections, enrich your career, improve your self-esteem, encourage you through life's tribulations and enhance your overall health. However, making poor friendship choices based on charisma instead of character is detrimental. Also, placing friendships in the wrong category can frustrate your life. I have discovered that friendships fall into about four categories. Failure to place your friends in the right category leads to misunderstandings and miscommunications.

Long Lasting Friends

Long lasting friendships weather many relationship storms as well as celebrations. Long lasting friends serve as safe havens for emotional transparency and intimate sharing. The fear of betrayal or a breach in confidentiality is oftentimes absent from long lasting friendships.

Generally these types of friendships can seem closer than your family relationships. They accept you unconditionally and are not afraid to tell you the truth in love. Long lasting friends challenge you to be your absolute best without being controlling or judgmental when you make mistakes in your life. In this type of friendship, you are free to be yourself without shame, compromise or apology.

Although you may not spend a tremendous amount of time with each other physically, the love, honesty, trust, loyalty, and yes even an occasional argument, keeps the friendship bonds strong. Long lasting friends are very intentional about making sure that the others' friendship needs are being met. They take the time to evaluate the relationship periodically and strive to improve the stagnant areas. In these types of relationships, individuals refuse to be fickle or phony friends. If you have at least one long lasting friend then you should consider yourself blessed.

Good Friends

Good friends can also be considered as your best friends. You have the same commonalities, shared values and moral ethics. Good friends usually look out for one another and support one another in public and in private. There is a willingness to share success but failures may be concealed until the comfort level has increased.

You may spend a lot of time with them however, you maybe apprehensive about sharing intimate details with each other. In this friendship it is sometimes difficult for you to speak truth without offense taking root. The level of trust and intimacy has not fully blossomed in this relationship but could if both parties are willing to put forth the effort.

Circumstantial Friends

Circumstantial friends are strictly based on the situations occurring in your life. These types of friendships are usually formed at work, church, school or professional organizations. They can also be formed because of a shared problem. Although you may spend more time with circumstantial friends, more so than your long lasting and good friends, there is a very small amount of emotional trust and connectedness developed.

There may be lots of laughter but loyalty is minimal outside of the circumstances in which the friendship was formed. Unfortunately, when the circumstances change, so does this friendship. Both parties may try to maintain the friendship outside the circumstances however these efforts more than likely are useless.

Casual Friends

Casual friends are usualy surface level friendships. No intimate information is shared neither is trust developed. There is absolutely no loyalty, commitment or disclosure of private information in casual associations. Having fun is the primary focus of these types of relationships. Once the fun is gone, this casual friendship is not far behind.

Episode 11:
Foolish Friendships

"Best friends are like diamonds, precious and rare.
False friends are like leaves, found everywhere."
—Anonymous

Friendships are difficult enough. But when you have to frequently endure the uncaring actions from a friend it is a clear sign that the friendship has turned into a foolish friendship. What are some signs to let you know that you are dealing with a fool? First of all, a foolish friend flaunts their accomplishments around with the sole purpose of trying to belittle you. They are full of negativity, drama and strife and happily infect your environment with the same. Lastly, a foolish friend seeks to be vindictive and vengeful when they do not get their way or you disagree with them.

Anyone of the four categories of friendships discussed in the previous chapter can unexpectedly turn into a foolish friendship. People change not only for the better but also for the worse. Nevertheless, do not let the length or depth of any friendship confuse you into thinking that you have to ignore a friend's foolishness for the sake of keeping the friendship.

I had to restructure a friendship that had become emotionally cancerous. After knowing Angie since elementary school, I realized that we no longer had similar values, goals or ethics. I was trying to hold on to the friendship simply because it was familiar to me.

The conversations were becoming increasingly toxic and unproductive. For example, every time I would share my goals of launching a newsletter or starting a life coaching business, Angie would doubt my ability to reach them. Snippy and condescending remarks would frequently spew from her mouth which always ignited a heated debate.

Yet instead of ending this increasingly cancerous friendship, I ignored it. I threw all my energies into my writing career so that I would have a legitimate excuse for being unable to hang out with her. But Angie quickly became a bigger distraction. She would intentionally call me on the days I told her were designated for writing my newsletter. "Girl, you can take a little break and go out to dinner can't you?" would be her tactic for distracting me. I had to remind her that I could not go because I was busy writing. Angie continued this tactic for months until I began to get serious about writing my first book *How To Deal With A Difficult Woman*. This time, I literally told her that I did not have time to hang out with her as much anymore because I was focused on finishing my book project. Two weeks after I established new friendship boundaries with Angie, shockingly she graciously respected them by giving me my space. Or so I thought.

Angie's friendship was becoming a toxic friend but I struggled with ending the friendship completely. I was ignoring the realities that our friendship was transforming into an unsupportive and emotionally draining situation. Subsequently, until I had reached my "enough is enough" point, I chose to stay stuck in a foolish friendship with Angie.

Episode 12:
A Not So Wonderful Change

*"For better or worse, you will eventually become more
and more like the people you associate with. So why not
associate with people who make you better, not worse?"*
—*Marie T. Freeman*

Seasons change and so do friendships. What once was a trusting,
fun-loving and productive friendship may grow into frustrating
agitations when one or more of the parties involved have not:

▶ Respected the boundaries that were set
▶ Addressed conflict, both spoken and unspoken
▶ Set realistic expectations
▶ Worked through personal insecurities, offenses or un-
healthy competition
▶ Confronted outside negative influences who have created
strife
▶ Examined shared values and belief systems

If these frustrations are continuously avoided then the friendships have no other choice but to become stagnant. Like stagnant water, stagnant friendships can develop a horrible relationship odor. If the odor lingers too long then the tension will become so thick that it will be next to impossible for the friendship to return to a harmonious state. On the other hand, some friendships need to be ended because they no longer satisfy the overall well being of one or both individuals involved. This was the case in my friendship with Angie whom I mentioned in the previous section.

As I stated, I finally reached my "enough is enough" point. Although Angie's unusual compliance of respecting my new friendship boundaries was a refreshing relief, I soon found out that it was slowly dividing another friendship that I cherished deeply.

While I was working diligently to finish my book, Angie befriended a close friend of mine named Heather. Angie and Heather began spending a great deal of time hanging out, going shopping and other social activities. It seemed as though they were forming a strong friendship bound, which totally baffled me because Angie and Heather were extreme opposites and had very little in common. But since I was so engrossed in my book project, I did not think too much about it. I was just glad that Angie no longer distracted me.

However, while I was pouring my love and attention into my book project, I failed to realize that I was neglecting my friendship with Heather. Although she never voiced her concerns about the change in our friendship, she found comfort in sharing them with Angie. How do I know? Because Angie would call me about every two weeks trying to masquerade her nosiness as a heartfelt prompting to persuade me to check on Heather.

But I did not fall for her trap because I knew that if Heather needed me for anything she would not hesitate to call me. Our friendship was much stronger than the one I had with Angie. Heather and I were more than two great friends who hung out together. Our friendship was a divine connection similar to the friendship that the biblical characters Mary and Elizabeth formed. We prayed together, interceded for one another and were spiritual accountability partners. Our friendship had endured death of parents, personal sicknesses and tremendous spiritual maturity.

Nevertheless, Angie's ploys magnified. Even though she knew that I had not talked to Heather, or anyone else for that matter in months, Angie's bi-weekly phone calls would always begin with the question, "Have you talked to Heather recently?" It took me many months to put the pieces together but Angie was calling me to stir up drama between me and Heather. She knew I had not spoken to Heather in months so she wanted to be the anchor woman on the "Heather's Weekly News Show."

"That's not true," was always my response to Angie. "You are lying. If that happened, Heather would have shared it with me." Eventually, I told Angie to stop calling me updating me on Heather's life. So even though I was ignoring my anger, which was festering because Heather had not alerted me of the drastic changes that were occurring in her life, I blew Angie's information off and continued finishing my book project.

Besides, I knew Angie always liked stirring up trouble anyway. I was familiar with Angie's exaggerated stories. But I never picked up the phone to call Heather to check on her and neither did she call to check on me. For almost a year, Heather and I communicated vicariously through Angie's biweekly updates.

The entire situation was surreal. I could not help but to conduct a mental rewind of similar friendships that Angie managed to drive a wedge between. Angie had always loved to play the "I know something about your friend that you don't know" mind games with people. Surely since we both were in the incubation stage of forty, her desire to play that game should have subsided. But it had not.

Convincing myself that I was too old to be a participant in Angie's immature friendship craziness, I still did nothing to address the situation. It had been almost two years and ironically my friendship with Heather had become almost nonexistent. Sure we did the cordial calls whenever we thought about it but nothing that would resemble the lasting friendship we had nurtured for almost ten years. I realized that I was caught up in a friendship rerun with Angie.

Angie had not only become toxic in my life but her poison had infected another one of my friendships. Florence Isaacs writes, *"Toxic friends are people who exhibit a pattern of damaging behavior and are rarely well meaning...Someone who harms you or those you love...is toxic."*

I accepted responsibility for the part I played in allowing Angie's toxic friendship to flourish into other areas. I should have ended the friendship months before because there were blatant signs of friendship dysfunction ringing out loud and clear. However, I chose to reject the truth and make excuses for tolerating Angie's behavior. My failure to address my feelings and calmly confront the silent conflict that was brewing has damaged both friendships.

Months of avoiding these negative emotions developed a root of bitterness, resentment and friendship regret that has been very difficult to heal from. This is exactly what happens when there is a communication breakdown between friends. There is no room for ignoring issues when difficulties arise especially in long lasting friendships. Communication is a crucial key to establishing acceptable boundaries and expectations, correcting concerns, destroying negative influences, avoiding offenses and misinterpretations.

REFLECTION EXERCISE
"FRIENDSHIP CHECK UP"

Because people change and friendships evolve, I have learned the value of doing a friendship assessment. Periodically you should examine your friendships by doing a check up. Identify the friendships in your life. Answer the below questions.

1. **Is the friendship pure?** Is the fundamental building blocks of the friendship free of hidden motives, jealousy, resentment, insecurities, strife, inadequacy or selfish physical and material gain?

2. **Is it positive?** Is there a balance of optimism, encouragement, praise, constructive criticism and willingness to give support without conditions? If not, when will you discuss this problem with your friend?

3. **Is it productive?** Is the friendship bearing emotional, physical and spiritual fruit? Are you a better person because of this association?

4. **Is it progressive?** Is the friendship growing to an intimate level of emotional support in which both parties are secure enough to be honest about their successes, fears, and failures? If not, what are the hindrances? How will you remove the hindrances?

Episode 13:
The ABC's to Healthy and Fruitful Friendships

"Life does not always turn out to be your fantasy. That is why you need friendships that are real to get you through it all"
—*Carrie Bradshaw (Sarah Jessica Parker) Sex and the City*

B y this point, it should be clear that friendships tremendously influence your self-perception, serenity and success. Therefore, friends must remember to practice their ABC's in the relationship.

Below are a few ABC's that should be evident in healthy and fruitful friendships.

A: Authenticity, Autonomy, Apologetic

Authenticity is the first key to fruitful friendships. I know that I have mentioned this word about a million times throughout this book but I can not stress this point enough. Discovering that a friend has not been real in word, personality or actions destroys trust. You feel betrayed when you realize that a friend has not been genuine. Authenticity in friendships creates strong friendship bonds even in the midst of conflict.

The next factor is to allow autonomy to flow throughout the duration of the friendship. Autonomy means being free to have a voice and a choice. Embracing autonomy encourages friends to be their authentic selves. Autonomy gives you the freedom to be wrong in the friendship without fear of rejection, judgment and condemnation.

Lastly, all friendships will have moments in which an apology is needed. Humbly apologizing for a wrong committed can be the difference between a fruitful friendship and one that is headed for failure. At the same time, the most productive friendships embrace a delicate combination of overt authenticity, genuine autonomy and timely apologies.

B: Belonging, Boundaries, Balance

Belonging is the 3rd level of Abraham Maslow's which was discussed early in the book. A sense of belonging creates emotional trust, security and a willingness to persevere through seasons of tension. Feelings of friendship insecurity, disloyalty and abandonment may be present in the absence of belonging.

Next, clear boundaries must be communicated so everyone will understand exactly what constitutes acceptable and non-acceptable friendship behavior. At a 2006 singles conference at New Birth Church in Atlanta, Georgia, Elder Bernice King, daughter of Dr. Martin Luther King, Jr., stated in a teaching seminar that *"Part of the reason why there is so much conflict in friendships, family, business and spiritual relationships is because people have not understood how to set boundaries."* Unnecessary anger, over commitments, resentment, avoidance and bitterness could be avoided if boundaries were established.

Finally, having balance both publicly as well as privately stimulates a stress-free friendship. A friend who does not practice balance in their individual life will more than likely overstep boundaries and bring chaos as well as unrealistic expectations to the friendship. In addition, all friendships must progress through the same stages of rest that was explained earlier in Episode 9. In addition, when people have other positive and fruitful associations outside the friendship, codependency issues may be eliminated.

C: Communication, Compassion, Conflict

Friends who can not have honest communication with each other may need to reassess their friendships. Fruitful friendships must progress from surface level conversation to a more in-depth exchange of hopes, dreams, fears and vulnerabilities.

Secondly, there must be a genuine display of compassion during misfortunes, mishaps and mistakes. Whether recovering from tragedies or enduring the consequences of a wrong decision, compassion can curb the enthusiasm of duplicating the same errors repeatedly. Thirdly, conflict is apart of the friendship life cycle. Conflict stimulates friendship maturation. Conflict is healthy when it is managed immediately.

In conclusion, applying the ABC's will create fruitful friendships. It is beneficial for you to flee friendships with those that become toxic. Healthy friendships should add value to your life. Fruitful friendships encourage each person to bear plums of maximized potential, oranges of optimism, melons of motivation, raisins of righteousness, pears of purity and strawberries of success. Now why would you even think about settling for less when you can choose friends who challenge you to be your absolute best?

REFLECTION EXERCISE
"DEFINING FRIENDSHIP"

1. Define what true friendship means to you.

2. List 5 values that you and your friend must share for you to consider them a friend.

3. Identify a friendship that you cherish. Based on your above definition and values, is the friendship healthy and fruitful? If not, what changes need to be made?

For more friendship assessments and reflection, please visit Tanya's Tips newsletter archive via www.tanyawhite.com to view issue# 100 with guest writer Jennifer Blair.

Series 3:
The Gospel of Christians Connections

"The church has always been the foundation that unified our communities. Like no other gathering, the assembly in the church house fostered an environment that permitted and appreciated self expression, liberation and creativity."
—*Rev. Nicole Barnes, Author of Restoration of the B.A.D. Girl*

P salm 133:1 the psalmist David writes that it is wonderful and pleasant for Christians to fellowship together in peace and harmony. But, unfortunately sometimes relationships between Christians are the most divided, stressful and discrediting relationships that one will ever encounter. Since the church is a place where one goes to find spiritual tranquility and unconditional love from other disciples, it is devastating when one has repeated relationships with Christians who demonstrate the direct opposite. Instead of creating heavenly hope, some Christian relationships are filled with hellish hoopla that taints God's divine design and purpose.

Episode 14:
But I thought You Were A Christian?

"Don't team up with those who are unbelievers. How can righteousness be a partner with wickedness? How can light live in darkness? What harmony can there be between Christ and the devil? How can a believer be a partner with an unbeliever?" (2 Corinthians 6:14-15)

This familiar scripture is usually only applied when selecting a marriage partner. Yet, the apostle Paul did not isolate this scripture specifically for couples. It was referring to all relationship categories. Paul made it clear in 1 Corinthians 5:9-10 that he did not mean for believers to separate themselves from unbelievers. On the contrary, he explained developing intimate and trustworthy relationships with people who claim to be believers, yet willfully indulge in explicit behaviors forbidden in the scriptures and rationalizing their ungodly actions should be prohibited. A believer who justifies their intentional sin not only harms themselves but infects the integrity and purity of the entire body of Christ.

Still, many believers repeatedly attach themselves to ungodly Christian connections by using Romans 3:23 as validation for ungodly Kingdom relationship reruns. It is imperative to understand that Sunday associations should not automatically constitute a legitimate and healthy personal friendship outside of the sanctuary walls. As Florence Issacs explains in her book, *Toxic Friends, True Friends*, friendship can be defined as *"a relationship of voluntary interdependence where two people get together because they want to and take a personalized interest in and feel concern for each other."* Sadly, a large number of relationships formed in church are based strictly on the persona that is witnessed in the context of the sanctuary walls without further investigation to see if there are any friendship compatibilities.

Attending the same church does not guarantee that you have the same values. Christians should accept that these are truly the days that are written about in 2 Timothy 3:1-9 (Amplified Version): *1-3 "But understand this, that in the last days will come (set in) perilous times of great stress and trouble [hard to deal with and hard to bear]. For people will be lovers of self and [utterly] self-centered, lovers of money and aroused by an inordinate [greedy] desire for wealth, proud and arrogant and contemptuous boasters. They will be abusive (blasphemous, scoffing), disobedient to parents, ungrateful, unholy and profane. [They will be] without natural [human] affection (callous and inhuman), relentless (admitting of no truce or appeasement); [they will be] slanderers (false accusers, troublemakers), intemperate and loose in morals and conduct, uncontrolled and fierce, haters of good.*

4-6 [They will be] treacherous [betrayers], rash, [and] inflated with self-conceit. [They will be] lovers of sensual pleasures and vain amusements more than and rather than lovers of God. For [although]

109

they hold a form of piety (true religion), they deny and reject and are strangers to the power of it [their conduct belies the genuineness of their profession]. Avoid [all] such people [turn away from them]. For among them are those who worm their way into homes and captivate silly and weak-natured and spiritually dwarfed women, loaded down with [the burden of their] sins [and easily] swayed and led away by various evil desires and seductive impulses.

7-9 [These weak women will listen to anybody who will teach them]; they are forever inquiring and getting information, but are never able to arrive at a recognition and knowledge of the Truth. Now just as Jannes and Jambres were hostile to and resisted Moses, so these men also are hostile to and oppose the Truth. They have depraved and distorted minds, and are reprobate and counterfeit and to be rejected as far as the faith is concerned. But they will not get very far, for their rash folly will become obvious to everybody, as was that of those [magicians mentioned]."

In a nutshell, the Bible is warning us that everyone who is faithful in church attendance is not always faithful in their allegiance to living a Godly life. You will recognize a committed Christian by the fruit they bear. If you are striving to live a righteous and holy life that is pleasing to God, then connecting with Christians who are double minded and who conform to ungodly lustful behaviors is not wise. These associations will eventually influence you to do the same.

People do not always participate in worship services for spiritual transformation. There are various reasons why people faithfully attend church. According to the book, *The Distinguishing Traits of Christian Character,* by Gardiner Spring, D.D., there are 7 forces that bring people to church and never become a committed Christian:

▶ The force of education
▶ The force example
▶ The force of public opinion
▶ The force of influence of erroneous
▶ The force of natural conscience
▶ The force of fear
▶ The force from the love of error

Tears do not bring about transformation. Confession does not equate to a changed life. There are some distinguishing characteristics that every authentic Christian should display such as love, forgiveness, loyalty, honesty, sexual purity, commitment to Godly standards, faithfulness, peace, uprightness and righteousness (2 Timothy 2:22, 1 Timothy 2:1-4, 1 Timothy 6:11-12, James 3:13-18, 1 Peter 1:13-25, Colossians 3:1-17, Leviticus 20:7-8). By these traits will you know that someone is a true disciple of Christ.

Authentic Christianity is not about lip service but about life service. You will know that someone is a Christian by their character which can not be manufactured. Focus on how great a person's character is instead of being swept away by their charisma when making Christian connections. Character separates the true disciples from the great pretenders.

Episode 15:
Socializing in the Sanctuary

"In order for you to progress, the Lord will give you some Kingdom connections. These connections are designed to push you forward and continue to build your confidence in who you are and what God has appointed you to do."
—*Reverend Syvoskia Bray, Author of It's In You: 12 Power Principles for Becoming the Woman God Called You to Be*

You should thoroughly research a person's reputation outside their church persona through observation, investigation and socialization before assimilating people into your inner Christian connections. Observe how people interact around other saints in the church and watch how people respond to them. If you notice that there are more negative responses than positive, do not make excuses or justifications. Dig deeper and ask the person questions. There is an abundance of relationship reruns that can be prevented if we would just ask questions.

As you are conducting your observation, also do an investigation. Who are they spending the majority of their time talking to? What group do they socialize with? Does the group have behaviors that reflect your same spiritual and ethical values? Lastly, your socialization with a person outside of church will reveal their true identity. God commands us to love our neighbor (Matthew 22:38-40). But God also warns us that bad company corrupts good character (1 Corinthians 15:33-34).

Episode 16:
Avoiding Godly Gangsters Posing as Spiritual Leaders

"Churches are meant to be safe places where spiritual leaders help and equip the members for the works of service. There are some churches however, where leaders use their spiritual authority to control and dominate others, attempting to meet their own needs for importance, power, intimacy or spiritual gratification. Through the subtle use of the right spiritual words, church members are manipulated or shamed into certain behaviors or performance that ensnares them into legalism, guilt and begrudging service."
—David Johnson & Jeff VanVonderen, Authors of The Subtle Power Of Spiritual Abuse

Godly gangsters? Isn't that an oxymoron? Maybe, maybe not. A gangster is someone who is affiliated with an organization whose activities are centered around pleasure, profit and power. These activities are executed through methods of intimidation, manipulation, extortion and bribery. If you were to randomly survey Christians to find out if they have ever felt intimidated, manipulated,

114

extorted and bribed by a spiritual leader, you may be surprised at the amount of people who answer yes.

Bishop George Bloomer boldly pinned it as authority abuse. David Johnson and Jeff VanVonderen call it spiritual abuse. Whatever the term, it is like Stage IV cancer eating away at the very heart of Christians. One minister, who spent five years serving under a spiritually abusive ministry, stated, *"At first I did not know what was going on. I had been in physically abusive relationships in the past. But being spiritually abused is worse than that. It still hinders me today. It has decreased my zeal for working in ministry and operating effectively in my God-given purpose."* Ministry leaders must recognize the harmful affects of misusing their Godly authority.

I still have faith to believe that the number of spiritual leaders who exemplify integrity, holiness, honesty and a Godly love for people far exceeds the number of those who are Godly gangsters. However, I will not ignore the grave repercussions that are occurring because the number of Godly gangsters prowling many pulpits today.

Bill Hybels writes in his book, *Courageous Leadership,* *"When the spiritual gift of leadership comes alive in churches everywhere, the church will become the hope of the world and a most influential force for good."* Unfortunately, the reverse is happening more often than it should. As a result, many Christians have decreased their church attendance, ministry involvement, questioned their belief in God, gotten distracted from their purpose or have turned totally away from the Kingdom of God primarily due to a Godly gangster who is posing as a spiritual leader.

How can Christians honestly know if they are under the influence of a Godly gangster? Sadly, the behavior is similar to that of physical and sexual domestic abuser. According to an article on domestic violence published by the Louisiana Coalition Against Domestic

Violence (LCADV), at the root of any abuse is the uncontrollable quest for power and control. The 8 behaviors given by the LCADV are outlined below and have been modified to reflect the traits of a Godly gangster:

▶ **Using coercion and threats:** Godly gangsters make and carry out threats to ruin people's reputations in the Christian community, strip them of positions or force the parishioners to engage in spiritually immoral and illegal acts.

▶ **Using economic abuse:** Godly gangsters constantly ask the congregation for money. Imposing guilt or rejecting the individuals who do not adhere to the financial demands becomes the standard of a Godly gangster.

▶ **Using male privilege:** This is when women are only viewed as servants while men make all the decisions concerning the operation of the church. Women have no real authority in their delegated positions.

▶ **Using children:** Godly gangsters use children to relay messages to the adults or mistreat children when the abused has not cooperated with the abuser.

▶ **Minimizing, denying and blaming**: Saying that the abuse did not happen or that the person is not a faithful Christian further fuels the spiritual abuse.

▶ **Using isolation:** This includes controlling what the person does outside of the abuser's sight, what they listen to, read, where they go and who they talk to other than the abuser.

▶ **Using emotional abuse:** Godly gangsters have frequent

episodes of belittling remarks, playing emotional mind games and humiliation towards the people who do not agree with their leadership style.

▸ **Using intimidation:** Most people are afraid of discussing negative feelings or experience remorse about thoughts of leaving the church when they are under ungodly leadership.

Other behaviors that accompany spiritually abusive situations are jealousy, controlling behavior, unrealistic expectations, hypersensitivity, rigid rules, verbal abuse and the "Dr. Jekyll and Mr. Hyde" syndrome. When someone is a Godly gangster it has a domino affect in the lives of both the abuser and the abused.

In scriptures such as Mark 9:42 and Proverbs 28:16, God makes it emphatically clear that those in authority have a responsibility to lead correctly or negative consequences will follow. If you examine the lives of such leaders as Saul (1 Samuel 9:1-31:13), Abimelech (Judges 9:1-57), and Haman (Esther 3:1-7:10), you will see how their Godly gangster mentality ended in their physical deaths while hundreds that followed them were left dead mentally, emotionally and spiritually.

So how can you protect yourself from repeatedly connecting with Godly gangsters posing as spiritual leaders? You must understand the qualities of a Godly leader. Godly leaders will exhibit the below characteristics:

1. **Have high moral and ethical integrity in word and deed—** There is nothing worse than a leader who does not have integrity. No leader can ever hope to make a positive impact if they do not have integrity in word and deed. Remember that people do not follow what leaders say but what they do. (Titus 1:5-9)

117

2. **Enlightens people and gives helpful advice**—Effective Godly leaders feed the minds and share spiritual advice with those who follow their leadership. (Proverbs 29:17, 2 Timothy 4:1-5)

3. **Embraces and develops peoples' gifts and talents**—Every Godly leader should gladly help to develop people's unique gifts by providing resources and opportunities for development. (1 Corinthians 12:1-31)

4. **Educates, equips and empowers people for works of service**—Whether it is formal or informal, the statement is true: *"Knowledge Is Power!"* Education equips people to be prepared for greater works of service. It empowers them to mature and be assured in their calling. (Ephesians 4:11-16)

5. **Offers opportunities for others to use their gifts**—Godly leaders serve as midwives to their followers' destinies. Godly leaders should always have suitable and growing opportunities for people to exercise their gifts. (1 Corinthians 12:1-31)

6. **Encourages people in both failures and successes without jealousy, judgment or condemnation**—Godly leaders are not afraid to speak the truth in love. They gently offer correction in love but they also acknowledge your successes. (Titus 2:1-7)

Once you have realized that you have been connected to unhealthy spiritual leadership then immediately seek God for healing, forgiveness and guidance. The Lord will let you know whether to confront the problem, leave the situation or expose it. The next step is to immediately seek Christian counseling and support. Do not hide the fact that the abuse has occurred. Like any abuse, talking about it will be hard at first. But God heals what we are willing to reveal. 1 John 1:9 says, *"But if we confess our sins to Him, he is faithful and just to forgive us and to cleanse us from every wrong."* Many times abusers have been abused themselves. So, you must pray for the abuser as well as the abused. Prayer is a stabilizer in a very difficult situation. The prayers of the righteous do availeth much!

Episode 17:
How to "Pray" for the Correct Christian Connections

"God determines who walks into your life, but it's up to you to decide who you let walk away, who you let stay and who you refuse to let go." —Anonymous

Recovering from an ungodly Christian connection can paralyze you from seeking further relationships in the church. Bitterness, resentment, regret and shame may try to sprout up but refuse to succumb to that anger trap. However, to escape another Christian connection rerun, you must pray about who you embrace into your intimate Christian circle.

When I say pray I am not using that as a nonchalant cliché but as an effective strategy to protect you from those Godly gangsters and other ungodly sanctuary predators. After you have conducted a thorough observation, investigation and socialization, determine if your Christian connections pass the **"PRAY"** litmus test for healthy Christian relationships:

▸ **P**—Does the person have **pure** motives for wanting to build a connection? Does the person possess a **positive** attitude about people and situations the majority of the time? Is the connection going to be **productive**? Is the person **polite** to others inside and outside of the sanctuary?

▸ **R**—Is the person **real** or are they pretending to be someone else? Are they striving to live a **righteous** life before God? Are they **responsible** in their professional and home life? When they have committed a wrong against someone or even God, are they **remorseful** or do they blame someone else or their situation?

▸ **A**—Is **abiding** by God's standards and commandments a priority or do they modify holy standards to justify their lifestyle? Are they **approachable** or are they spiritually arrogant isolating themselves from people who are not on the same spiritual, economical and social level? Is it easy for them to **apologize** when they are at fault or does pride overtake them? When in various social settings are their actions **amicable** or do people always find them unfriendly and hard to get along with?

▸ **Y**—Do they **yield** to the will of God for their life or ignore it because it does not fit into their plans and desires?

The relationships you form in church impacts your spiritual maturity and ultimately our God given destiny. Christianity is not a title but a lifestyle.

REFLECTION EXERCISE
"PRAY FOR YOURSELF"

1. Use the "PRAY" model to assess whether you are a fit Christian connection. Honesty is the best policy. Be specific. List a corrective action plan for areas where you fall short.

Series 4:
Working 9 to 5

*"Never continue in a job that you don't enjoy. If you're happy in
what you're doing, you'll like yourself and have inner peace.
And if you have that, along with physical health, you'll have
more success than you could possibly have imagined."*
— *Roger Caras*

In her 1980 smash hit song *9 to 5*, off the soundtrack of the movie
of the same name, Dolly Parton summed in up perfectly that the
worst position to be in is to have an unappreciative, intimidated
and money hungry employer. An employer who never gives you credit,
always ignores your devotion, wants you to remain stagnant and
never encourages you to move ahead, can literally drive you crazy.
Consequently, haphazard job hopping oftentimes produces workplace
reruns. It is imperative that you learn how to properly confront difficult
job issues and remind yourself why you are at work in the first place.
This will greatly reduce the chances of you falling into another
unsatisfying job situation.

Episode 18:
Facing Guerilla Warfare in the Workplace

*"There are rules to follow and rules
to make, know the difference."*
— *Armando Montelango of "Flip This House"*

According to a press release sent out on February 23, 2007, by The Conference Board via www.conference-board. org, less than half of all Americans have reported that they were dissatisfied with their jobs. There is a plethora of reasons for this widespread job dissatisfaction such as being overworked, underpaid, underappreciated, and being in an unpleasant working environment. Because of all of the reasons listed above, sometimes the workplace can feel as though you are in the middle of guerilla warfare.

Does your workplace have you in a constant state of agitation? Has your job become professionally unsafe and hostile towards employees? Does your boss engage in a barrage of small attacks on employee performance and ability? If so, then you may be in the midst of guerilla warfare in your workplace.

Guerilla warfare is an unconventional method based on sneak attacks carried out by small groups of people. These tactics encourage sabotage, espionage and deception. Guerilla warfare groups ambush their targets and oppose mass confrontation. Also, these groups frequently win their battles by spreading propaganda, instituting sudden unexplainable reforms and executing terrorist type actions. The primary goal of guerilla warfare is to destabilize the environment so that it becomes extremely vulnerable for an easy takeover. This is what Ginny endured on her new position in the management trainee program.

Ginny had been accepted into one of the most competitive management trainee programs at one of the largest banks in her city. Recently graduating with her Master of Science degree in Finance, this program was Ginny's next career step on her journey to become Chief Financial Officer of a bank. Ginny had to work at various branches and departments in order to master each function of banking. Within weeks, Ginny was receiving accolades from every department manager she worked with. However, when Ginny was assigned to Anna's branch, the accolades turned into accusations. For the first time in her career, Ginny found herself in the middle of an unpleasant work environment.

Ginny's boss, Anna, was about twenty years her senior. Anna did not have a formal college education but worked her way through the ranks of banking to become branch manager during her twenty-five-year tenure with the company. Anna had a leadership style which included employee intimidation, espionage and favoritism. She had her two office spies who reported employee complaints to Anna on a daily basis. Anna was infamous for reprimanding coworkers for irrelevant job concerns such as not participating in after work team building social activities, not volunteering to coordinate community events and not decorating the branch every month with the designated holiday theme.

Ginny never met a person that she could not connect with. Being the quintessential team player, her departments always seemed to be stress-free particularly because Ginny was extremely optimistic and motivating. So from the moment Ginny reported for duty at the branch, she became Anna's next target of constant criticism. Ginny had to endure Anna's low employee performance evaluations, senseless weekly reprimands, added responsibilities without being given the resources to effectively complete the tasks and professional slander amongst other managers that Anna conversed with at the bi-weekly district meetings.

For the first time in her career, Ginny was experiencing job dissatisfaction. She could not comprehend why Anna was thoroughly displeased with everything she did. Ginny was deeply wounded by Anna's attacks and irrationally concluded that banking may not be her calling. Ginny was on the verge of quitting the management trainee program until she decided that succumbing to temporary guerilla workplace warfare would delay her professional aspirations. She had to put on her workplace war clothes until she completed the management trainee program. Within a few years, Ginny was promoted to district branch manager. Imagine how Anna felt when she was told that Ginny was now her boss.

When you realize that you are in the middle of harsh criticism constantly, there are several strategies that are sure to help you endure the office manure:

1. **Accept that you are in the middle of workplace warfare and protect yourself.** Once you have witnessed guerilla warfare tactics in your workplace then accept it. Workplace warfare is

126

real. So protect yourself. Beware of office cliques, department gossip and group alliances. Workplace guerilla troops know their ultimate objective and will achieve it by any means necessary.

2. **Realize that no one is safe under guerilla warfare attack**. Guerilla groups will lie, make excuses and even find loopholes to fit their personal agenda. Expect job sabotaging, inconsistent implantation of policy procedures and frequent complaints to the boss about your performance.

3. **Plan your strategy**. Do not be hasty about retaliating against workplace warfare troops because you will loose every time. Instead, devise a clever offensive plan of action. Sharpen your professional skills. Diversify your career plan and seize new opportunities. Never put all of your eggs in one basket, especially with an organization that has exhibited guerilla warfare tactics in the past.

Unfortunately, what many employees once considered a home away from home has become a professional haven of hell. Gird up your professional loins of knowledge and skill so that you can survive your 9 to 5.

Episode 19:
How to Calmly Confront Career Criticism

"You can't always focus on the negative things people say about you in life. All you can do is go and enjoy the game."
—*Donovan McNabb*

One Sunday, during my weekly ritual of personal reflection and rejuvenation, I watched an inspiring interview with quarterback Donovan McNabb on *Real Sports*. McNabb has endured a barrage of negative critiques ever since he was the second-round draft pick for the Philadelphia Eagles. Despite his impressive performance record, such as being named to the All Pro team five times, leading his team to four conference title games and exhibiting a unique brand of class and dignity off the field, McNabb's credentials are frequently found in the conversation slaughterhouse.

Donovan McNabb is an exemplary model of how to calmly handle constant career criticism. I discovered that although constant career criticism is disheartening, coping with the negativity is possible when you remember to:

128

1. **Continue to show up for the game.** Never let anyone's negative opinions force you to abandon a career that you love. Sadly, no matter how much good you do there will always be negative comments. Muster up the strength to continue to show up for the game and ignore the naysayers.

2. **Play your position with consistent excellence.** In the midst of any stressful workplace, do not allow discouragement to deter you from performing your best. Try to be committed to a habit of excellence by any means necessary.

3. **Stick to the real issues.** Addressing issues that are irrelevant to your level of performance is useless and only creates additional frustration. Always stick to the subject at hand.

4. **Be humble enough to admit weakness and develop a plan of improvement.** You should analyze the message behind the method of criticism. If there is some validity to the criticism then develop a personal plan of improvement.

5. **Refuse to have irrational outbursts as a means of retaliation.** Do not give your critics the satisfaction of loosing your cool. Always show them respect and remain calm even in the midst of their hurtful attacks.

6. **Resist the temptation to try to prove yourself.** Your critics will always have something negative to say no matter how great your accomplishments. You will be wasting energy spending time on trying to prove your worthiness to them.

7. **Create a confident and trustworthy support system.** It eases your stress when you know that you have a few people who defend you publicly and privately when everyone else seems to be against you.

129

Enlist a support system (preferably off the job) of people whom you can trust. You need to feel emotionally safe so that you can honestly discuss concerns and receive an objective advice.

Episode 20:
Connecting the Disconnection Between Employers and Employees

"It's YOUR responsibility to make YOUR dreams a reality."
—*Les Brown*

One of the primary reasons why so many people are unsatisfied with their jobs is because of the huge gap between the level of employer expectation and employee dedication. Employers who hold on to the philosophy that adequate salary and benefits are enough to satisfy their employees are really in for a rude awakening. According to an August 2007 Labor Day survey, reported on www.kronos.com, 62% of employed adults are either currently actively or passively looking for a new job. With these overwhelming statistics, it is wise that employers seriously examine how to satisfy and retain their current employees especially when it reportedly costs 150% of an employees' base annual salary to replace them.

In an April 2008 *Black Enterprise* magazine article entitled "Here's What I'm Looking For," a survey conducted by the Spherion Corporation proves that employers are clueless as to what is important to employees and vice versa. For example, factors such as benefits, compensation and growth and earnings potential were viewed as the top three out of eight job motivators by employees while the same three motivators were ranked number four, five and six on what employers viewed as essential benefits from the employers' perspective. This huge disconnection explains why employee loyalty, job satisfaction and performance continue to rise throughout many organizations today.

Communication is the key to connecting this employer and employee disconnection. Employers must realize that the days of an employee staying on the job for fifteen, twenty or thirty years are rapidly becoming extinct. The emergent employee demographics and attitudes have drastically changed from that of the traditional worker of the baby boomer generation. Trudy Bourgeois states in the "Here's What I'm Looking For" *Black Enterprise* article *"The baby boomer generation was rooted in a pay-for-time mentality; today's workforce wants a pay-for-performance mentality."* When there is no compromise of the two mentalities, the workplace suffers. An employer who has embraced the pay-for-time mentality and has an employee base operating from the pay-for-performance mindset can usually expect excessive employee absenteeism, turnover, office tension, low morale and low productivity.

What Employers Can Do to Connect the Employee Disconnection

Employers can connect the disconnection by first being open to instituting authentic change which has a balanced benefit for both employer and employee. Of course employers should analyze compensation and benefits that are equal to the employees' education, job expectations and equitable to industry standards. Implementing strategies such as performance bonuses and profit sharing programs are not only incentives for increasing employee productivity and retention, but these employee compensation improvements do so without adding a financial burden to the company.

But at the same time, employers should review non-monetary areas such as:

▶ **Balanced work load**—Nothing decreases the morale and motivation of an employee quicker than overloading them with work and having unrealistic deadlines. Balance eliminates employee pressure, increases productivity and eventually enhances company profits. Job sharing, modified work weeks and flexible work hours are awesome ways to address unbalanced work loads.

▶ **Respect for personal life**—Employers, especially those who have an extreme pay-for-time mentality, can forget that employees have a life outside of work. Employers should not expect employees to prove their loyalty and company dedication by always having them work overtime, requiring attendance at after hour's company functions and strongly persuading them to volunteer for non-work related community activities. When an employee has a balanced work and personal life it increases job morale, productivity and retention.

Creative strategies that companies can implement to show respect to their employees' personal life is by planning occasional after work social outings, becoming a sponsor of a selected employee charity or acknowledging non-related community and family achievements such as running in a marathon, winning a talent contest or a child's graduation or sports achievement.

▶ **Culture/work environment**—How do your employees interact with one another? Are there too many chiefs leading and not enough Indians who follow? Do your employees feel safe enough to express an opinion without being black-balled or being viewed as a troublemaker? Are your employees disrespectful towards each other? Do they discredit their peers job performance? If so, are you a supporter of this destructive office behavior?

Employers who do not promote a peaceful and non-threatening work environment create unhealthy work relationships between their employees. Unhealthy corporate cultures are plagued with fragmented team efforts, petty employee disagreements and high incidents of office conflict. Unfortunately, when employers are confronted with employee conflict they either avoid the issue or accuse the employee without doing an unbiased and thorough investigation of the issue.

Oftentimes, the employee conflict is usually a result of the clashing of employee personalities instead of incompetent employee performance. Conflict over personalities adds tension to the company culture and environment. Investing in diversity training, conflict resolution and workplace etiquette training will transform a stress-filled office into a stress-free operation.

▶ **Opportunities for career growth and advancement**—No one wants to feel trapped in a boring job. Encouraging your employees to grow and expand their professional knowledge can be extremely lucrative to your company's profits. Offer personal and professional development trainings within your company that will enhance your employees overall growth. Also, give deserving employees new titles and responsibilities. Change is often a refreshing improvement for a disgruntled employee. Lastly, employers should offer a tuition reimbursement program so that employees can increase their professional knowledge and marketability. Employers would be shocked as to how loyal employees become when there is a vested interest shown in their career development.

What Employees Can Do to Connect the Employer Disconnection

While employers are doing their part there are also some strategies that employees can implement to connect the relationship disconnection. Although circumstances may warrant legitimate job unhappiness, employees still have a responsibility to do the job that they were hired to do. Employees should be committed to give their employers effort, efficiency, effectiveness, loyalty and results regardless of the frustration they may feel.

Episode 21:
How to Make the Most Out of the Job You Have Until You Find the Job You Want

"The people who succeed in this world are the people
who get up and look for the circumstances they want,
and if they can't find them, they make them."
— *George Bernard Shaw*

B ishop T.D. Jakes proclaimed in his book, *Ten Commandments of Working in a Hostile Work Environment*, that your job is not a place where you seek social acceptance or activity. It is an outlet in which you perfect your God given assignment and receive a financial reward. Your job is not obligated to make you feel happy. Neither is your job required to fulfill your social needs. You are at work to get a paycheck. Anything other than that is a bonus.

At some point, everyone has hated their current job situation. Workplace warfare brings about frequent frustration. Constant career criticism creates continual agitation. But until you land the job you want you must make the most of what you have. You can tolerate the mess on your job as soon as you practice the following habits:

1. **Avoid internalizing second hand information.** Within a hostile work environment the office gossip is usually operating at maximum velocity. Employees are sharing information about management. Management is listening to hearsay about employees. Even though nothing has been confirmed openly, most people add fuel to the fire when they internalize second hand information. As tempting as it is to believe everything you hear in the office, resist being lured into office hearsay that has not been confirmed by the proper authority channels.

2. **Respect the boundaries of the employer and employee relationship.** According to the author of *Toxic Friends, True Friends,* Florence Issacs, *"It's very hard to be personally close with someone over whom you have power or who has power over you."* A great number of employees and employers have gotten burned professionally because they have misunderstood the boundaries of friendship on the job.

3. **Consistently increase your marketability.** Employees should avoid the trap of limiting their professional skills and knowledge. Increasing your marketability in the job market may include you pursuing a college degree, obtaining certifications, participating in training and development courses. In addition, you should be an active member of several professional networking organizations. Meeting other professionals in a safe and purposeful setting also allows you to build your professional exposure. Most people tend to land their dream jobs through word-of-mouth inquiries at professional networking organizations.

137

4. **Create a diverse career contingency plan.** Diversifying your career opportunities may mean that you continuously assume new responsibilities or apply for new positions. In addition, be open to maximizing your opportunities to generate multiple streams of income. *Essence* magazine calls this having a "side hustle." You can turn your pastime into a profit so that you can switch roles from employee to entrepreneur.

REFLECTION EXERCISE
"LANDING THE JOB YOU REALLY WANT"

1. Describe your ideal job in the following terms:
   - Location
   - Salary
   - Benefits
   - Vacation and sick leave
   - Retirement or investment opportunities
   - Community involvement
   - Advancement and promotion opportunities
   - Training and educational opportunities
   - Leadership philosophy and style

2. List 3 ways you can increase your job marketability and design an action plan for each.

3. Update your resume or executive profile. Start researching positions that fit your ideal job terms and send your resume.

Series 5:
Strictly Business

"One of the major challenges facing entrepreneurs and business leaders is finding the right business partners. Great care should be exercised when selecting associates because the wrong choice can harm the reputation and earnings of your company."
— *William R. Patterson, Author of the National Bestselling Book, The Baron Son*

Business wonders can quickly transform into business blunders when you are involved with unprofitable resources. Business transactions with honest, morally upright and customer friendly professionals are essential to generating financial profits.

Episode 22:
Before You Say "Yes" See What Saying "No" Will Show

"Question your motives before spending money. Make sure you spend your money in a way that reflects your vision and purpose."
—Valorie Burton, Rich Minds, Rich Rewards Newsletter

We have all been romanced by a slick salesperson that uses flattery or friendship to convince us to purchase something that we really did not need, want or could afford. Do not get duped into a bad business transaction that will devastate you financially. Stay alert when talking to salespeople who are charismatic or who use aggressive closing techniques.

I was reminded of this fact when I was contacted by Becky, a radio salesperson about a new business opportunity. "I received an e-mail about your new book, *How To Deal With A Difficult Woman*, and I wanted to talk about booking you for one of our radio shows," was the message that Becky left on my phone. Excited that someone almost 2,000 miles away wanted me to be a guest on a radio show, I did not hesitate calling her back.

She hesitantly revealed her true motive for contacting me which was a little bit different than she originally stated. "I really wanted to talk to you about possibly hosting your own internet radio show with our company," Becky explained. "I normally do not tell people what I really want because they get freaked out."

"Me, host a radio show? I don't think I am ready for that," I replied even though hosting my own radio show was on my marketing plans for the upcoming year. I thought this was a divine opportunity that God was dropping in my lap. But I have never been so wrong.

Becky's confidence in my professional skills and prediction for huge success were unexpectedly gratifying. She was impressed with my website and had reviewed some of my previous newsletters. I was ecstatic because she was so willing to help me increase my newsletter subscribers and my media exposure a hundred fold. She even showed her immediate support by signing up for the newsletter, requesting a review copy of my book and pitching me several great show ideas for this new radio venture.

But when I started asking her more in-depth questions, especially concerning the radio show costs, her previous angelic patience rapidly transformed into hurried anxiousness and a very skillful diversion. This salesperson, who just days earlier was extremely sweet and encouraging, morphed into a short-tempered tiger. Strategies of intimidation, belittlement and threats of me loosing the opportunity of a lifetime began to be the foundation of her sales pitch. She also had the audacity to convince the CEO of the internet radio station to call me with further bullying tactics.

Upon her last efforts to persuade me to invest in my own radio show,

Becky's silent anger dominated her tone of voice when she saw that I was not going to pursue the deal. She immediately began feeding me the infamous "If you don't act now, the deal will not be available when you are ready" line. As I zoned out of her last ploys of persuasion, a sense of relief infiltrated my mind because her true colors were shining through. After about thirty minutes of her aggressive sales techniques, I finally told her that I was not interested in the radio venture. The next day, ironically she deleted herself from my Tanya's Tips database.

Despite this unfortunate bump in the road, I learned some vital life lessons of what saying no to aggressive sales people can really show. Saying no when you are not completely convinced that something is right for you can reveal:

▸ **The real motives behind sales people's actions**—If business people get upset and resentful when you say no, you may want to question their business approach. Anyone who genuinely wants to do business with you understands the importance of having repeated business from a customer. Politeness and patience should be evident when a salesperson is trying to attract a new customer. They should want to build a business relationship with you even when you tell them no because you are able to offer them referrals.

▸ **The prevention of future relationship tension and stress**— A sales person who manipulates, intimidates or slanders your character when you tell them no is slowly uncovering a little bit of what will come in the future of your business relationship.

Episode 23:
How to Protect Yourself From Financial Molestation

"If you say yes when in your heart you truly want to say no, then you will always be trapped in a dismal closet of chaos, compromise and incompleteness."
—Tanya White

About six months later, after the radio show disaster, another salesperson named Sam left me a message about forming a strategic business partnership. "I saw your business profile on the business on-line website. I would love to talk to you about us forming a strategic partnership so that we can both expand our coaching cliental." Once again, my curiosity was peaked and I called him back immediately.

I quickly discovered that the real reason for Sam's call was for me to become one of his business coaching clients. His reasoning was that I first needed to master my sales techniques so that I could start generating thousands of dollars from coaching clients like he did. "After I teach you some star sales techniques, we can form a strategic partnership," Sam persuaded. "But until then, I will let you coach a few sessions with my clients and pay you a minimal fee." Of course, my portion was only about 3% of what he charged. Nonetheless, I entered into a coaching agreement with Sam without researching his client success rate. After all, I really needed to improve my closing techniques for my coaching business to increase my profits.

Within the first couple of sessions, I found out a few disturbing things about my new sales coach who was going to help me earn thousands of dollars. First, I had been coaching longer and had more experience in the field of coaching than Sam. He was not at all experienced in coaching, as he led me to believe. In reality, Sam's background was in sales and not coaching.

Secondly, his sales approach was manipulative. Sam confessed that he tailored his conversations, promises, affirmations and questions based on some proven sales color personality chart. Basically, everything he told me about developing a partnership, and the faith he had in my ability, were empty affirmations. He had no intention of forming a business partnership with me. I felt pimped and dreaded every coaching session from that point on. I ended the coaching contract a few sessions after Sam's unpleasant confession. Although these may be guaranteed sales strategies, hearing his tactic to lure me in to becoming his sales coaching client made me feel hustled or for a better clarification, financially molested.

Now before you get confused, please let me explain what I mean by financially molested. The definition of molested is to be subject to unwanted or improper activity. Although the term is usually referring to a sexual act, discovering that Sam intentionally lied and lured me into a deal that was inappropriate—based on my level of expertise and experience—and was very similar to the profile of a child molester, according to www.childluresprevention.com. He coerced me into a financial obligation that made me feel used and abused monetarily. You may totally disagree with me equating that experience with molestation, but honestly that is exactly how I felt.

Yet, unlike a sexual molestation, I could have prevented falling into this trap if I did not ignore the signs that this was not a productive business relationship. The profile of a financial molester is as follows:

▸ Tells creative lies to make a sale by any means necessary.

▸ Pressures you into making a quick decision.

▸ Uses aggressive, intimidating or belittling tactics to coerce you into doing business with them.

▸ Excessively contacts you for a decision.

▸ Offers creative payment plans even after you have told them you are not financially able to pursue business transaction.

▸ They play on your ignorance promising that you will make lofty financial gains.

▸ They use affection or genuine concern to lure you into closing the deal with them.

Any of the above tactics should be red flags that something is out of sync with your deal. Before you make your final decision, utilize the below three strategies that I should have implemented before signing on a client with Sam:

▸ **Contact previous or former client referrals**—Ask the person for previous written client testimony. Legitimate business people have clients whom you can contact by phone or e-mail for referral purposes. Whichever works for you, always ask the business professional for a client testimony. If they refuse, then do not give them your business.

▶ **Do not make a decision too quickly**—You do not need to make any immediate decisions about spending your money. It's **YOUR** money! You have the ultimate authority as to how and when you will spend **YOUR** money. Contrary to what many aggressive sales people might tell you, you will not miss any imaginary once in a lifetime deal if you refuse their offer. Be patient when making spending decisions.

▶ **Be leery of too many probes into your personal life**—Business relationships should always remain strictly business. Business professionals who want to dig too deep into your personal life more than likely are trying to discover your vulnerabilities and emotional weakness. They want you to make an irrational emotional buying decision whether you truly can afford it or not.

Remember that business is business. Do not succumb to tactics of intimation and manipulation. Use patience and wisdom when contemplating a financial purchase.

Episode 24:
Picking Profitable Partners

*"No person will make a great business who wants to
do it all himself or get all the credit."*
— Andrew Carnegie

P icking profitable partnerships in business endeavors can either multiply or mess up your organizational growth and reputation. Large company revenues should not be the only determining factor when looking for business partnerships. An elite rolodex will not guarantee a successful business connection. Nor will a person's great excitement and unending commitment result in partners producing effective results. Every business leader should be encouraged to consider the important factors before solidifying partnerships.

Selecting profitable partnerships involves that all parties have the:

▶ **Same Mission**—Being on the same organizational page makes for a more effective and efficient partnership. Strife, stress and division are drastically reduced when individuals have the same mission and are passionate about fulfilling it.

▸ **Sincere Motives**—Impure motives produce impure actions. Involvement in a partnership for reasons such as seeking social acceptance, jealousy, revenge or the opportunity to interact with people you admire quickly leads to frustration, low commitment level and intermitted results.

▸ **Spotless Morals**—Whatever is done in someone's private life will adversely affect their business life. Questionable acts such as infidelity, inappropriate sexual conduct, mistreatment of people or misappropriation of funds are actions that taint the overall reputation of the organization publicly.

▸ **Steadfast Methods**—The old cliché which says that "Quitters never win and winners never quit" applies to selecting partners. It is beneficial to have partners who stick with you in the good, bad and ugly times of the organizations' development.

▸ **Smart Money Matters**—The end goal of any business is not only to have enough money to generate a profit but ultimately companies expect to have additional dollars to invest in its expansion. This requires sound financial decisions that monitor expenditures, savings and investing.

Picking profitable partnerships demands that you make wise choices. Whether you are soliciting volunteer help for your ministry or searching for financial investors to fund your business, select individuals who can add value to your brand image, keep organizational peace and multiply your profits.

REFLECTION EXERCISE
"HANDLE YOUR BUSINESS"

1. For excellent business coaching exercises and information, please visit www.baronseries.com.

Series Finales: It's Never the Right Time to Say Goodbye

"If you can't change the people around you, then change the people around you."
— *Mark Gunn, Radio Personality, Radio One Louisville, Kentucky*

Goodbye. Farewell. Adios. Au revoir. In no matter what language, saying goodbye to things that are familiar and comfortable to us is extremely difficult to do. Oftentimes we can make saying goodbye to some friendships, jobs, relationships or even business partnerships an episode straight off of Days of Our Lives. However, relationship goodbyes do not always have to be a negative event. On the contrary, goodbyes are frequently a mandatory pre-show to one of the most productive seasons of your life. You could save yourself a tremendous amount of positive energy if you embraced the gift of goodbye so that you rid your life of unhealthy, unproductive and unsatisfying relationships.

Episode 25:
8 Simple Rules for Breaking the Emotional Chains that Bind You to Relationship Reruns

"A girl can wait for the right man to come along,
but in the meantime that still doesn't mean she can't
have a wonderful time with all the wrong ones." — Cher

At this point, I pray that you have been strengthened and encouraged to finally let go of the relationship reruns in your life. Having the wrong person in a right relationship paralyzes your divine purpose and confuses your emotions. Stop making irrational relationship decisions for satisfying feelings of loneliness, pacifying issues of rejection or escaping reality.

Break free from forming microwave relationship that quenches your emotional, spiritual and physical needs temporarily. Subsequently, these types of connections are satisfying for a short time but they will never give you the nourishment ultimately needed to sustain the longevity of the relationship. Instead, place your relationships in a slow cooker so that they can simmer to perfection. When you allow your relationships to develop and mature at a slower pace then they will leave a sweet aroma that permeates throughout every area of your life.

Applying the below 8 simple rules will place you on the path to experience satisfying, stress-free and significant relationships.

Rule 1: Discover and embrace your authentic self.

Be committed to discovering who you really are without any titles, professional accolades, social status, material trappings or activities you are associated with; self discovery requires intentional alone time. Begin a journey of personal awakening so that you will have a clear understanding of your likes, dislikes, desires, personality and abilities.

Furthermore, getting in touch with the real you compels you to not only work on your areas of improvement but allows you to celebrate the good parts of who you are. Remember, if you do not love your authentic self then you will always compare your life to others. In addition, you more than likely will develop an attitude of defeat that drives you to live your life frequently seeking affirmation and approval from others. Knowing and loving who you really are ignites a level of self-confidence that becomes contagious. Self-confidence attracts the right people to you and decreases the occurrences of relationship reruns in your life.

Rule 2: Know what you stand for and refuse to apologize or explain it.

Discover your purpose, mission and standards for your life. Knowing what you stand for stems from discovering your authentic self. Ask yourself, "What are my moral, ethical, spiritual, religious, relational, financial and political standards?" Once you have developed life standards that are acceptable to you then refuse to apologize for it. Remember, it is your life! Choose to live it the way you want to according to your moral and spiritual beliefs.

153

Rule 3: Heal from painful issues from your past.

Healing is critical to maintaining healthy relationships. Unresolved pain births insecurities and codependency issues in your relationships. Wounded people attract wounded people. Seek the counseling, therapy or life coaching to overcome your past pain.

Rule 4: Understand the reason for and the season of each relationship.

Everyone who enters your life comes for a reason and a season. You must identify the reason for each one of your relationships. Ask yourself the following questions:

▸ What is the purpose of this relationship?

▸ Is the purpose going to enhance or hinder my life?

▸ Is this person compatible with my moral, ethical and spiritual standards?

Rule 5: Establish and communicate relationship boundaries and expectations.

You cannot fault others for overstepping boundaries that they never knew existed. Communicate your relationship boundaries and consequences for crossing these boundaries. Have a firm understanding of the other person's boundaries and expectations. However, when someone does not adhere to your relationship boundaries and expectations please do not automatically end the relationship. Simply restate your boundaries and establish firm consequences if they are violated again. Remember, you can verbally tell people your boundaries all day long. But if you do not live the boundaries you set then others will not abide by them either.

154

***Rule 6: Confront relationship conflict calmly, honestly and
immediately.***

The quickest way to invite tension and nurse resentment is to dodge
relationship conflict. Conflict is not always a negative sign. Most
conflict can be resolved calmly and immediately. Healthy conflict
usually strengthens the bounds of the relationship. Important tips to use
when you confront conflict in your relationship include the following:

▸ Determine whether the conflict is legitimate or is it a result of
  displaced anger, abandonment, rejection and other unresolved
  personal issues. If it is the latter, reread Rule #3.

▸ Pick a time to discuss the legitimate conflict issues when your
  emotions are not escalated. This only invites irrational words
  to be said usually creating permanent relationship damages.
  Select a time of peace as well as a place that is not emotionally
  threatening or intimidating where you can openly and honestly
  discuss the conflict.

▸ Listen carefully to the other person's perspective instead of
  being so anxious to voice your concerns.

▸ Speak assertively without being too aggressive. Since conflict
  is very uncomfortable to address, most times people will use
  strategies such as avoidance, blame or introducing irrelevant
  issues to wander away from the subject. Should this happen,
  try redirecting the conversation back to the original issue.
  Maintain your focus. In addition, use "I" statements instead of
  "you" statements to eliminate anyone feeling attacked, belittled
  or judged.

▸ Remember the goal of addressing conflict is to create a solution.

155

Shun using the time to vent anger or address issues irrelevant to the conflict at hand.

▶ Accept the fact that there may be times when the only solution to conflict will be to distance yourself from the relationship or to end it completely. You must know when to hold them and know when to fold them.

Rule 7: Be very cautious who you allow into your intimate circle of influence.

After dealing with several episodes of relationship reruns you should be more cautious of who you allow into your intimate circle of influence. Relationships are an earned privilege not an inalienable right. Make people earn the right to be a part of your life by monitoring such traits as their dependability, trustworthiness, loyalty, level of integrity and respect for boundaries.

Rule 8: Consistently live a life of truth, integrity and balance.

Truth is being honest, genuine and real in word and action. Integrity is demonstrating the moral and ethical conviction to be honest, whole and present a reputable character both privately and publicly. Lastly, balance is the ability to live a life of stability. These three characteristics send a message to people as to how they can approach you in relationships.

From this moment forward, I challenge you to invest more time thoroughly observing the people you desire to form relationships with. Abandon the philosophy that relationships are suppose to be hard in order for them to be worthwhile. Relationships can be very easy and drama free when you apply the above 8 simple rules. Investing the time to analyze a person's behaviors, attitudes and compatibilities in the beginning of any relationship is a small price to pay compared to the costly investment you make emotionally, physically or financially for being in the wrong relationship.

If you have not gleaned anything from this book, remember this important relationship lesson: Your life is too short, too precious and too significant for you to keep selling yourself short by clinging to repeated cycles of unhealthy love connections, unsatisfying friendships and Christian connections, unwanted jobs and unproductive business relationships. You have the power to attract healthy, productive and satisfying relationships.

Stop settling for less than God's best for your life. Break the emotional chains that are keeping you bound to the vicious cycle of relationship reruns. From this day forward, be determined to have the right people, in the right relationships, at the right time and for the right reasons.

Relationship Reruns Recap: 30 Golden Nuggets for Guaranteed Relationship Success

Before you begin your new season of applying the strategies in this book, below is a brief recap of how you can break the cycle of choosing the wrong people for the right relationships. I believe that there are 30 golden nuggets that will guarantee that you have relationship success.

Specific To All Relationships

1. Be your authentic self!

2. Overcome past relationship hurts and offenses because you will attract what you have not been healed from.

3. Ask detailed questions before committing to developing any relationship.

4. Pay attention to people's actions because they really do speak louder than their words.

5. **When people show you who they really are believe them without excuses!**

Specific To Love Connections

1. Determine what type of person satisfies you spiritually, emotionally, financially and physically. Once you have a dating framework embrace it. Do not be ashamed or apologize for it.

2. Do not confuse a person needing you for them loving you.

3. Avoid living out a fantasy.

4. Refuse to compromise your moral, ethical and spiritual values to hold on to a love connection that makes your feel shameful and remorseful.

5. **When people show you who they really are believe them without excuses!**

Specific To Friendships

1. Place each friendship in the proper category to avoid confusion and unnecessary hurt.

2. Discuss friendship commonalties, shared values, establish boundaries and expectations.

3. Confront conflict and offenses calmly and immediately.

4. Protect your friendships and accept the seasons of change.

5. **When people show you who they really are believe them without excuses!**

Specific To Christian Connections

1. Esteem genuine Christian character over exciting church charisma.

2. Avoid being unequally yoked to unbelievers in your intimate circle of influences such as mentors, counselors, marriage partners, friendships and business associates.

3. Walk out the Christian principles that you shout about.

4. Be very prayerful before sharing intimate information with others.

5. **When people show you who they really are believe them without excuses!**

Specific To Working Relationships

1. Do not make money your primary determinant for accepting or leaving a job.

2. Thoroughly research a company before accepting a job.

3. Remember that your job is primarily a place where you receive payment. Friendships at work are secondary.

4. Diversify your professional opportunities and marketability.

5. **When people show you who they really are believe them without excuses!**

Specific To Business Relationships

1. If you cannot afford it, then do not buy it. You have the ultimate authority as to how you spend your money.

2. Refuse to allow your financial fallacies to force you into irrational and unprofitable business purchases.

3. Connect with profitable partnerships.

4. Be cautious of mixing business and pleasure without establishing clear boundaries. Remember business is business.

5. **When people show you who they really are believe them without excuses!**

Relationships are not hard as society wants people to believe. They are relatively easy when everyone involved remains committed to being truthful with themselves and the other person. You must be determined not to settle for less than God's best when developing relationships.

Join me on this new journey of breaking the cycle of choosing the wrong people for the right relationships. Make the commitment today to start embracing healthy, productive and satisfying relationships in every area of your life. End your season of relationship reruns. It is your time to begin a new season of enjoying relationships that are rated R for being real, relevant and refreshing!

Notes

Preview Section

1. Dr. Lance D. Watson, *Maximize Your Edge: Navigating Life's Challenges* (New Kingston, PA: Whitaker House Publishers, 2001), 96

2. Reverend Syvoskia D. Bray, *It's What You Crave* sermon, Bethel Baptist Church Women's Conference (Louisville, KY: 2008)

3. Napoleon Hill, *Think and Grow Rich* (New York, NY: Fawcett Book, 1988), 86.

Series 1 Section

1. http://en.wikipedia.org/wiki/Maslow's_hierarchy_of_needs

2. Dr. Robin L. Smith, *Lies at the Altar: The Truth About Great Marriages* (New York, NY: Hyperion Books, 2006), 23

3. http://www.census.gov

4. Myles Munroe, *Single, Married, Separated & Life After Divorce* (Shippensburg, PA: Destiny Image Publishers, Inc., 1992), 21,23

5. Dr. Jamal Bryant, *Foreplay: Sexual Healing For Spiritual Wholeness* (Durham, NC: Blooming House Publishers, 2004), 15

6. Michelle McKinney-Hammond, *Get A Love Life: How to Have a Love Affair With God* (Eugene, OR: Harvest House Publishers, 2000), 75.

7. Dr. Robin L. Smith, *Lies At The Altar: The Truth About Great Marriages* (New York, NY: Hyperion Books, 2006), 21

8. Shannon Ethridge, *Every Woman's Battle: Discovering God's Plan for Sexual and Emotional Fulfillment* (Colorado Springs, CO: Waterbrook Press, 2003), 35

9. Bishop George Bloomer, *Looking For Love: Building Right Relationships In a Not-So-Right World* (New Kingston, PA: Whitaker House Publishers, 2004),122-124

10. http://www.coping.org/relations/fantasy.htm

11. Michele Lanton, *Women's Journey To Wellness* (Prospect, KY: Professional Woman Publishing, 2007), 174

12. Stephen Arterburn, *The Secrets Men Keep: How Men Make Life and Love Tougher Than It Has To Be* (Franklin, TN: Integrity Publishers, 2006)

13. John Maxwell, *Relationships 101: What Every Leader Needs To Know* (Nashville, TN: Thomas Nelson, Inc., 2002)

14. Valorie Burton, *Why Not You: 28 Days To Authentic Confidence* (Colorado Springs, CO: Waterbrook Press, 2007), 45

15. http://www.truthaboutdeception.com/catch_cheating/public/signs_of_infidelity.html

16. http://www.womensaccounts.com/dating_a_loser.html

17. Dr. Phil C. McGraw, *Love Smart: Find The One You Want-Fix The One You Got* (New York, NY: Free Press, 2005), 75

18. Ian Kerner, Ph.D., *Be Honest-You're Not That Into Him Either: Raise Your Standards and Reach For The Love You Deserve* (New York, NY: HarperCollins Publishers, 2005), xix

Series 2 Section

1. http://www.oprah.com/xm/rsmith/200612/rsmith_20061201.jhtml

2. Florence Issacs, *Toxic Friends-True Friends: How Your Friendships Can Make or Break Your Health, Happiness, Family and Career* (New York: NY: Kensington Publishing Corp., 1999), 16-17

3. Elder Bernice King, *Are You The Ones* Singles Conference, New Birth Church (Atlanta, GA: 2006), Audio CD #603-175

Series 3 Section

1. Florence Issacs, *Toxic Friends-True Friends: How Your Friendships Can Make or Break Your Health, Happiness, Family and Career* (New York: NY: Kensington Publishing Corp., 1999), 2

2. Gardiner Spring, D.D., *The Distinguishing Traits of Christian Character* (Phillipsburg, NJ: Presbyterian and Reformed Publishing Co., 1999), 14-15

3. Bill Hybels, *Courageous Leadership* (Grand Rapids, MI: Zondervan, 2002)

4. http://www.lcadv.org/what%20is%20DV.htm

Series 4 Section

1. http://www.kronos.com/About/pr_LaborDaySurvey_aug28. htm

2. Kingsley Kanu Jr., "Here's What I'm Looking For!: Employees and Management Still Disagree On What Is Important," *Black Enterprise,* Volume 38, No. 9, April 2008, 70

3. Florence Issacs, *Toxic Friends-True Friends: How Your Friendships Can Make or Break Your Health, Happiness, Family and Career* (New York: NY: Kensington Publishing Corp., 1999), 25

About The Author

TANYA WHITE is the author of the bestselling book *How To Deal With A Difficult Woman*. A sought after life success coach, consultant and workshop facilitator, Tanya's exhilarating presence compels men and women to kick down the doors of ordinary living to transcend greater levels of personal and holistic success. While teaching Bible study classes for almost ten years to Christian singles, at one of Louisville's largest African American churches, Tanya inspired men and women to boldly fulfill their destiny through cultivating healthy relationships with God, themselves and other people. To date, Tanya has been featured in the 2007 and 2008 editions of the *Who's Who of Black Louisville* business directory, the 2008 premier issue of *Elect Lady Magazine* in an article entitled *25 Beautiful and Successful Singles* and in the 2003 *Today's Woman magazine* article entitled *Wise Decisions*. She also serves as the Communications Director for the Women's Evangelical Network (W.E.N.). Tanya resides in Louisville, Kentucky.

—

Men and women throughout the United States and in London, United Kingdom are inspired weekly from Tanya White via her e-newsletters. To subscribe to her free e-newsletter called *Tanya's Tips* or to book Tanya for your next event, order other products, register for teleseminars or life success coaching sessions, please visit www. tanyawhite.com.

MORE GREAT BOOKS BY TANYA WHITE

RELATIONSHIP RERUNS:
BIBLICAL BREAKDOWN STUDY GUIDE
and SPIRITUAL AWAKENING JOURNAL

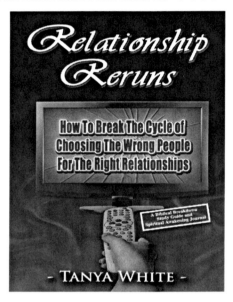

What happens when Godly people pursue ungodly relationships? How is the Kingdom of God really impacted when the redeemed of the Lord not only say so, but show so it through their dating relationships, friendships, work relationships, Christian connections and business partnerships? This book which is a great tool for group or individual study includes scriptural study, discussion questions, practical life applications and a spiritual awakening journal section. Available via www.tanyawhite.com, bookstores and online retailers.

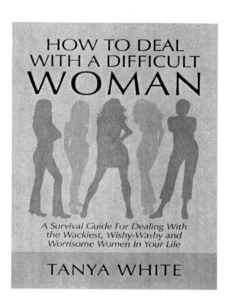

From the feisty females in your family to your obnoxious coworker, at some point or another you have asked the question, "Why does she act like that?" In *How To Deal With A Difficult Woman* Tanya White cleverly introduces you to 55 humorous profiles of some of the wackiest, wishy-washy and worrisome women who tend to disrupt your day in one way or another because you can't always ignore her, you can't always argue or avoid her. Eventually, you will have to deal with her. This book made the *Top 50 Black Christian Book Distributors Bestsellers List* several times in 2008. Available via www.tanyawhite.com, bookstores and online retailers.

Printed in the United States
137084LV00002B/4/P

9 780981 684703